ISBN 978-1-332-21549-2
PIBN 10299419

1 MONTH OF
FREE
READING

at

www.ForgottenBooks.com

By purchasing this book you are eligible for one month membership to ForgottenBooks.com, giving you unlimited access to our entire collection of over 700,000 titles via our web site and mobile apps.

To claim your free month visit:

www.forgottenbooks.com/free299419

English
Français
Deutsche
Italiano
Español
Português

www.forgottenbooks.com

Mythology Photography **Fiction**
Fishing Christianity **Art** Cooking
Essays Buddhism Freemasonry
Medicine **Biology** Music **Ancient**
Egypt Evolution Carpentry Physics
Dance Geology **Mathematics** Fitness
Shakespeare **Folklore** Yoga Marketing
Confidence Immortality Biographies
Poetry **Psychology** Witchcraft
Electronics Chemistry History **Law**
Accounting **Philosophy** Anthropology
Alchemy Drama Quantum Mechanics
Atheism Sexual Health **Ancient History**
Entrepreneurship Languages Sport
Paleontology Needlework Islam
Metaphysics Investment Archaeology
Parenting Statistics Criminology
Motivational

CARTIER SAILS THE ST. LAWRENCE

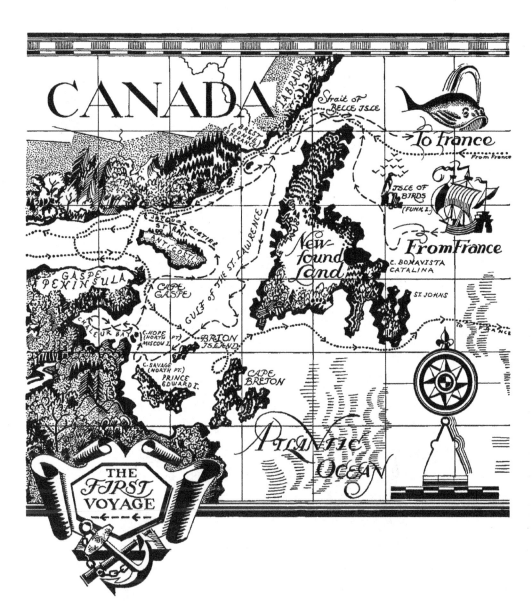

CANADA

LABRADOR

Strait of BELLE ISLE

To France

From France

BREST BONNE FRANCE

ISLE OF BIRDS (FUNK I.)

New-found Land

C. BONAVISTA
CATALINA

JACQUES CARTIER
STRAIT
ANTICOSTI I.

GULF OF THE ST. LAWRENCE

ST. JOHNS

GASPE PENINSULA

CAPE GASPE

CHALEUR BAY

C. HOPE (NORTH PT.)
MISCOU I.

BRION ISLAND

TO FRANCE

C. SAVAGE (NORTH PT.)
PRINCE EDWARD I.

CAPE BRETON

ATLANTIC OCEAN

THE
FIRST
VOYAGE
←←←

CARTIER
SAILS THE
ST. LAWRENCE

RETOLD BY ESTHER AVERILL

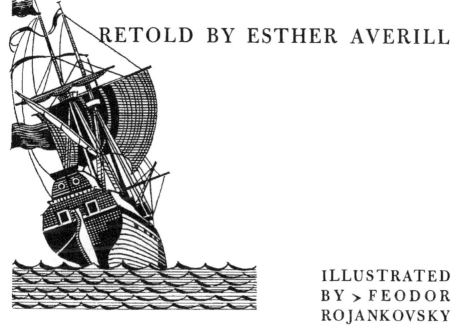

ILLUSTRATED
BY > FEODOR
ROJANKOVSKY

HARPER & ROW, PUBLISHERS, NEW YORK AND EVANSTON

Library of Congress catalog card number: 56–5159

CONTENTS

FOREWORD

AS FAR AS WE KNOW, THE EVENTS AND THE CONVERSATIONS IN THIS STORY ARE TRUE. THEY ARE TAKEN FROM THE LOGBOOKS OF JACQUES CARTIER AND FROM OTHER HISTORICAL DOCUMENTS OF HIS TIME.

By "logbooks" we mean the "original narratives" which were written from Cartier's own records of his voyages. It is believed that parts of the original narratives were written by Cartier, and other parts by a person, unknown to us today, who based his text on Cartier's logbooks. To simplify matters, these narratives are referred to in our story as the logbooks of Cartier.

Like real detectives, modern historians have searched the European libraries, the town records, and the old secret papers of the kings for scraps of information which have contributed greatly to our understanding of these voyages. We are especially indebted to the research work of Dr. H. P. Biggar, a Canadian historian, who has written two books which we have used as source material through the courtesy of his publishers, the Public Archives of Canada. The first of these books is *The Voyages of Jacques Cartier,* published with translations and notes; the second, *A Collection of Documents Relating to Jacques Cartier and the Sieur de Roberval,* from which we have gathered many of the facts in our chapter on the Portuguese spy, the King of France, and the Emperor of Spain.

THE FIRST VOYAGE

THE FIRST VOYAGE

THE NORTHWEST PASSAGE
TO CHINA

The people of St. Malo had built their town on a granite island close to the north coast of France. The island was surrounded by a sea, and the sea was an arm of the great uncharted ocean, the Atlantic, which covered the world in the west.

The force of the Atlantic pulsed through the sea and could be felt in the tides at St. Malo. Twice each day a galloping tide rushed toward the town and covered the white beach where the sailboats had been lolling on their sides. Sometimes the tide rose as high as fifty feet and hurled its waves against the granite walls that protected the town. Tides such as these taught boys to use their wits in handling a boat. It is no wonder that St. Malo became famous for her seamen.

In 1491 there was born in St. Malo a boy destined to take his place among the great sea captains of the world. His name was Jacques Cartier. Of Cartier's early life no trace can be found today. But the times in which he lived and the historical events that shaped his thoughts have been well recorded.

It was the period when men felt a pull toward the West—an urge to navigate the long-dreaded Atlantic. The urge was prompted by a new and exciting theory that the earth, instead of being flat like a table, is round like a globe. If that be true, a person might sail westward around the earth and eventually arrive in the East, in the coveted lands of silks and spices.

Men in west Europe, unaware of the true size of the earth,

3

believed that a western route to the East would prove much shorter than the long and dangerous eastern route. But Columbus, who led the westward search when he sailed from Spain in 1492, was thwarted by a strange new world, the world of the Americas, which loomed on his course. And none of the navigators who followed in his wake succeeded in reaching the East, because the huge continent of South America blocked the way.

The hope of finding a quick sea route to Asia shifted to the northern part of North America. John Cabot, for one, believed that in those northern waters, up where the earth's circumference diminishes as it nears the pole, could be found the short western trade route of which men dreamed. This trade route, or passage, came to be known as the Northwest Passage to China.

In 1497, when Jacques Cartier was still a small boy in St. Malo, Cabot set sail from England to seek the Northwest Passage. His voyage, however, ended in an icy region which was afterward called the New Lands, or Newfoundland.

Cabot's discovery of Newfoundland failed to interest most Europeans, since he brought home with him no gold or other treasure. But the merchants of St. Malo pricked up their ears on hearing his report that the waters off the ocean coast of Newfoundland abounded in codfish. France was a Catholic country whose people needed fish to eat on meatless days. So the St. Malo merchants began to send fleets each spring to the fishing grounds, or Banks, off Newfoundland. It is likely that Jacques Cartier, along with other young men of the town, accompanied some of these transatlantic expeditions. But of this we cannot be sure.

Of Cartier's early voyages, we know only that he once sailed in a Portuguese ship that crossed the South Atlantic to Brazil.

4

Columbus, Cabot, *Da Gama*, and Magellan were among the navigators whose voyages made men aware of the bigness of the world. Each of the four navigators sought a sea route to Asia.

Columbus sailed from Spain and stumbled upon the American islands.

Cabot sailed from England and discovered Newfoundland.

Da Gama sailed from Portugal, battled his way around the southern tip of Africa and up through the Indian Ocean to India.

Magellan sailed from Spain to the southern tip of South America, where he struggled through a perilous strait to the Pacific Ocean. He died in the Philippine Islands, but a few of his surviving men, with one of his ships, continued to sail westward and after rounding the southern tip of Africa returned to their home port in Spain. The first voyage around the world had been completed. It had taken three long years.

Apparently the warm southern regions of the New World, in spite of their riches, did not captivate him. His ties were with the North Atlantic, whose wild arm of a sea beat at the walls of St. Malo.

When, at the age of forty-three, Cartier suddenly entered the pages of written history, he held in his hand a commission from his king, Francis the First. The commission authorized Cartier to sail to Newfoundland and in the name of the King to search the waters beyond Newfoundland for the Northwest Passage to China.

How Cartier won the King's consent is not known today. Francis, unlike the kings of Portugal and Spain, had been slow to send explorers to the New World. Probably Brion-Chabot, the Admiral of France, who signed the commission, had helped Cartier obtain it. The commission was dated October 31, 1533.

Thirty-six years had elapsed since Cabot tried vainly to reach China by way of Newfoundland. Since then, several expert navigators from Spain and Portugal had attempted and failed to penetrate the region. Some of them had vanished forever on those wild and icy fogbound seas. Newfoundland, beyond the Banks, remained a dreaded area where most sailors feared to venture.

Even the merchants of St. Malo, though they respected Cartier's knowledge of the sea, felt he was planning a mad voyage. They failed to appreciate that impulse of his, that inexplicable urge to sail beyond the known horizons of the world. Besides, Cartier would need sailors and ships which they themselves would like to use. So the merchants made it impossible for him to obtain ships and a crew.

Cartier finally appealed to King Francis. And in March the King declared that no merchant should fit out a fleet before Jacques Cartier had equipped his own.

Cartier chose two small vessels, each of sixty tons' burden. They were wooden vessels, typical of the times, which means broad of beam, with high poop deck and two or three masts rigged with wide, square sails. His crew numbered about sixty men, and the ships were stocked with provisions to last from April until early fall.

Spring, with its easterly winds, was the best time to sail westward. On the twentieth of April 1534, Jacques Cartier left St. Malo on the outgoing tide. In twenty days the wind blew his ships across two thousand miles of sea and ocean, and he sighted Cape Bonavista on the east coast of the island of Newfoundland.

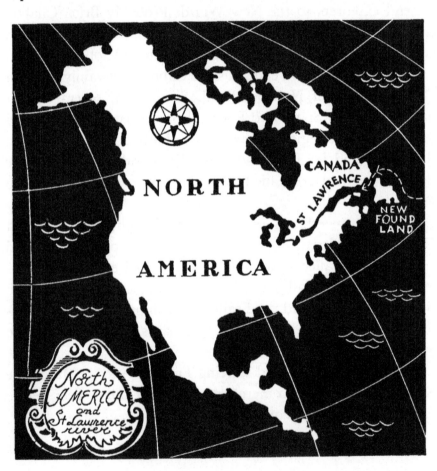

THE ISLE OF BIRDS

The stiff east winds which swept Cartier so rapidly across the Atlantic had driven masses of Arctic ice against the Newfoundland coast. Cartier was obliged to navigate a few miles south of Cape Bonavista and take shelter in Catalina Harbor, where he waited ten days for the winds to change and the ice to clear. Then he sailed toward the northern tip of Newfoundland.

His course led him along the border between the known and

the unknown regions. Here in the mists and the fogs and in the
ice-capped seas there still lingered (so most Europeans believed)
the fantastic creatures of medieval legend.

Those creatures were usually the frightening kind: hideous
monsters and fire-spitting demons that symbolized man's fear
of the unexplored seas. But one famous old legend, the *Voyage
of St. Brandan*, described the Newfoundland region in happier
terms. For the *Voyage of St. Brandan* expressed man's hope that
somewhere westward from Europe, toward the far horizon
where the sun set nightly in a blaze of glory, lay a land worth
finding.

In the mind of the Irish monk, St. Brandan, the promised
land in the west was the earthly Paradise which God had re-
served for His blessed ones. St. Brandan's quest led him from
Ireland to the cold waters which Cartier was now navigating.
In these waters, so ran the legend, St. Brandan discovered a small
island known afterward as the Isle of Birds (now called Funk
Island), where thousands of snow-white birds sang matins and
vespers and told him of their dreams and visions. St. Brandan
was so delighted that he remained there seven weeks. During
all that time his only nourishment was the singing of the birds.

In Cartier's day the island was known to a few fishermen who went there from the Banks to kill birds for food. But an air of mystery still hovered around the rocky ledges. Not until Cartier arrived had there been anyone to view the island with the eyes of a naturalist and report accurately on what he saw. Here is Cartier's description of the Isle of Birds, taken from his logbook:

The birds are there in such great numbers that it is unbelievable unless you have seen it. Although the island is about a league in circumference, it is so very much filled with birds that they look as if they had been stowed there. Roundabout and in the air there are a hundred times as many as on the island. Some are as big as geese, and black and white, with beaks like a crow's, and they are always in the sea, without ever being able to fly, for they have small wings, about half a hand in length, with which they skim as quickly through the water as other birds do through the air. And these birds are so fat that it is a marvelous thing.

We call them apponats [great auks], and in less than half an hour we loaded our two longboats with them as if they were stones. On each ship four or five casks of them were salted down, aside from those we could eat fresh.

There is also another kind of bird which goes both in the air and sea. These are smaller and are called godez [tinkers], and they place themselves under the protection of the larger birds.

There are others even larger, and they are white and stay by themselves in another part of the island, and they are vicious to attack, for they bite like dogs, and are called margaulx [gannets].

Cartier's account of the Isle of Birds is characteristic of his logbook as a whole. Accuracy of observation is the dominant note, and from his entries we can reconstruct his course and follow him as he sails his two ships over the uncharted waters of the New World.

Of the daily routine aboard the ships he makes no mention. But now and then he records some little incident which would indicate that life was not dull for his crew. His account of a bear chase near the Isle of Birds gives evidence of this:

Although this island is fourteen leagues from shore, bears come here from the mainland [Newfoundland] to feast upon the birds. Our men came upon a bear as big as a calf and white as a swan, leaping before them in the sea. On the following day, which was Whitsuntide, as we were travelling toward land, we found this same bear about midway, and he was swimming toward land as quickly as we went with our sails. Having sighted him, we chased him with our longboats and seized him by force, and his flesh was as good to eat as that of a two-year-old heifer.

THE GULF OF ST. LAWRENCE

From the Isle of Birds, Jacques Cartier proceeded to the northern tip of Newfoundland, which is separated from the forbidding coast of Labrador by the Strait of Belle Isle.

It was spring when Cartier turned west and entered the Strait. It was the time of the year when the great waters beyond Newfoundland free themselves of ice and push their broken ice packs east toward the Atlantic. Gigantic icebergs, beautiful to behold but dreaded by all sailors, ride through the Strait to join the ocean.

Cartier picked his way carefully through this turbulent onrush of ice. Sometimes he went in a longboat to explore the Labrador coast, though he could see there little but cragged rocks and stunted trees and moss. "I should say this is the land God gave to Cain," he wrote in his logbook.

A band of roving Indians he met seemed to him to lead a miserable life in this bleak region. He said:

They have fine enough bodies but are a hideous and savage lot. They knot their hair on their heads like a handful of twisted hay with a nail or some other thing passed through the middle, and woven in are the feathers of birds. These natives, men and women alike, clothe themselves

15

CANADA

LABRADOR

Strait of
BELLE ISLE

BREST
(BONNE E.)

To France

ISLE OF
BIRDS
(FUNK I.)

From France

New
found
Land

C. BONAVISTA
CATALINA

JACQUES CARTIER
STRAIT

GULF OF THE ST. LAWRENCE

GASPE
PENINSULA

CAPE
GASPE

WILBUR BAY

C. HOPE
(NORTH
MISCOU I.)

BRION
ISLAND

C. SAVAGE
(NORTH PT.)
PRINCE
EDWARD I.

CAPE
BRETON

ATLANTIC
OCEAN

THE
FIRST
VOYAGE
←-←-←

in pelts, but the women are more wrapped in their pelts and are belted
at the waist. They all paint themselves with tawny colors. They have
canoes in which they go to sea, made of birch bark, and from which they
catch many seal.

By the tenth of June Cartier had brought his two ships safely
through the Strait of Belle Isle and had reached the harbor of
Brest, now called Bonne Esperance, which is ninety miles from

the Atlantic. This was the last western port of which Europeans had any common knowledge.

Cartier remained at Bonne Esperance for almost a week. During that time his men stocked the ships with fresh food and water, while he himself went in a longboat and explored the coast for about twelve leagues toward the west. One day he chanced upon a large French fishing vessel whose pilot had lost his way. Cartier boarded the vessel and guided her to safety in a nearby harbor. Then he returned to his own ships.

On the fifteenth of June Cartier left Bonne Esperance and headed south along the west coast of Newfoundland, which has a length of about three hundred miles. He was now sailing on a vast, uncharted expanse of water that was believed to be a bay. Cartier, at this point, had no way of knowing that he was on the gulf of one of the world's great rivers, the St. Lawrence.

As Cartier sailed down the Gulf of St. Lawrence he had to fight his way through heavy mists and fogs. His only instruments of navigation were the crude ones then in use: the compass, the cross-staff, and the astrolabe.

The compass gave the points North, South, East, and West, while the cross-staff and the astrolabe served to determine latitude, or the north-and-south position of a ship. Both the cross-staff and the astrolabe were hand instruments which a pilot used for astronomical observation. Under the best conditions they were liable to an error of fifty or sixty miles. In a heavy gale, when the ship rolled and the wind slapped the instruments, the readings could err by as much as three hundred miles.

Longitude, or the east-and-west position of a ship, was an almost hopeless problem. Time and speed must be calculated scientifically if longitude is to be determined. But in Cartier's day, time on shipboard could be told only by hourglasses filled with dribbling sand. Nor was there an accurate method for measuring a ship's speed. A captain never knew the exact distance his ship had run during a day. However, it has been said that the early navigators, like Cartier, had a feel for the sea—an instinct that took the place of scientific equipment.

On the twenty-fourth of June Cartier reached Newfoundland's southwest headland, Cape Anguille. Then he turned southwest on the Gulf of St. Lawrence to search for the Passage to China.

Summer had come, and the green islands he discovered made a pleasing contrast to the bleak coasts he had left behind. A thrill of joy may be detected in the simply written pages of his logbook. Of one particularly beautiful island, which he named Brion Island, in honor of the Admiral of France, Cartier had this to say:

This island is the most excellent land we have seen, for two acres of it are worth more than all the New Lands [Newfoundland]. We found it filled with splendid trees and heaths, fields of wild oats and flowering pease as thick and as fine as I ever saw in Brittany and which seem as if planted there by farmers. There are many gooseberry bushes, strawberry plants, Provins roses and other good, strongly-fragrant herbs.

On Brion Island the sailors found bears, foxes, and many other animals known to Europeans. However, there was one strange creature, the walrus, which few Frenchmen had ever seen. Cartier had difficulty in describing it; he said clumsily that it was like a large ox and had two tusks, like an elephant.

Two of the sailors were sent in a longboat to seize a walrus that was snoozing on the shore. But when they drew close, the beast awoke and slipped away through the water.

As Cartier sailed over the southern waters of the Gulf of St. Lawrence, he named the islands and the other noteworthy places after prominent French people or the Catholic saints. But to one headland (the present North Point on Prince Edward Island) he gave the name Cape Savage in honor of a lone American

18

Indian who had stood there beckoning to the sailors. The Indian, however, grew alarmed when they rowed toward him and he fled. The sailors left two presents for him: a European knife and a woolen girdle hanging on a tree.

Woolen girdles, scarlet caps, bright red necklaces, and knives and hatchets were among the articles Cartier had brought with him from France. He planned to trade these with the inhabitants of whatever lands he touched. He hoped, of course, that he might soon arrive in China.

On the fourth of July Cartier reached a headland (North Point on Miscon Island) which he named Cape Hope, because to the north he could see highlands running toward the northwest. Between the highlands and Cape Hope lay miles and miles of glittering water which seemed to say, "This is the route to China."

The air was so warm and balmy that a sailor might well imagine he could smell the scent of Asiatic spices in the wind. He might dream that he could see in the far distance the bright golden roofs of some great palace of the Chinese Emperor. But the men who went in longboats to explore the stretch of water brought back the discouraging news that this was only a very deep bay. Cartier called it Chaleur Bay, meaning Bay of Heat— a name suggested by those hot days in July.

FRANCIS I

LAND FOR THE KING OF FRANCE

What was this land that lay between Jacques Cartier and China? What was this wilderness he had discovered? It had no European name. It did not exist on any map. He could not know that the waters of Chaleur Bay lapped the mainland of what is now called Canada.

Cartier anchored his two ships in a cove of the bay and went off in a longboat to explore the neighboring shores. He found that the land toward the south was flat and would make good farm land. The land toward the north, now called Gaspé Peninsula, was a highland covered with a forest of wonderful trees; among them, cedars and spruces that would make good masts for ships of three hundred tons or even more.

While Cartier was reconnoitering in his longboat, a fleet of

20

about fifty Indian canoes slipped into the bay and surrounded him. Although the Indians made signs of friendship, Cartier was afraid to trust them. He shot two small cannon over their heads, and this made the Indians draw back. After a while they returned, and he discharged two fire lances (long sticks filled with explosive powder). This time the Indians kept at a distance.

Next day the Indian chief came to Cartier's ships with nine canoes. The Indians waved pelts from the ends of sticks until Cartier went in a longboat and gave the chief a bright red cap and exchanged knives and hatchets for the pelts.

The following day three hundred Indians—men, squaws, and children—crowded the shore. They bartered their furs and all that they owned until they were naked. But more valuable to

Cartier than the Indian furs were two native words which he learned and entered in his logbook:

cochy: which means hatchet
bacan: which means knife

He wished to collect as many Indian words as possible so that he might make a useful glossary of them.

On the twelfth of July Cartier returned to the Gulf of St. Lawrence. After several days of violent storms, he entered Gaspé Bay. Here he met another band of Indians who were on a fishing trip, and they amazed him by their way of living with almost no possessions. In his logbook he observed:

This tribe may really be called savage, because it is the poorest tribe there can be in the world. All of them together have not the value of five sous, aside from their canoes and fishing nets. They go entirely naked, except for a small skin with which they conceal their sex, and other old pelts which they throw over themselves for scarves. They are not of the same nature or language as those we met before. They have their heads shaved all around, except for a bit on the top of the head which they leave long like a horse's tail and which they tie and knot on their heads with leather. They have no other lodging but their canoes which they turn up and sleep under on the ground. They eat their meat nearly raw after they have warmed it slightly on the coals, and also their fish . . . They are marvelous thieves and steal everything they can.

Cartier gave the Indians many gifts, including knives and hatchets, combs, tin rings, and bells. The Indians were delighted.

And now the time had come for Jacques Cartier to observe a practice common among European explorers. This wilderness he had discovered must be claimed for his king. On the twenty-fourth of July Cartier erected a giant cross on the headland at Cape Gaspé. The shaft rose thirty feet in the air and the crossbar stretched out its long arms as if to claim possession of

the surrounding lands. Beneath the crossbar hung a shield engraved with the fleur-de-lis of France. Above the shield, on a wooden bar, were carved the words:

LONG LIVE THE KING OF FRANCE

In the shadow of the cross the sailors knelt in prayer. Then they pointed to the sky and made the Indians understand that the cross was also a symbol of religion. The Indians gazed in silent admiration.

But afterward, when the Frenchmen were aboard their ships, a chief paddled toward them in a canoe with three of his sons and a brother. The chief would not come so near as usual and from a distance began shouting. He pointed to the cross and with his two fingers formed a similar cross, and by other signs made it clear that he was saying, "This land belongs to me. You have no right to plant the cross without my permission."

Cartier paid no attention to these protests. His mind was busy thinking up a scheme for taking the chief's two sons to France. European explorers often carried home a few Indians as curiosities to show the kings. Cartier had a second reason for wishing the chief's two sons to go to France. While they were in France, they could learn to speak French. Then they would be able to act as interpreters if he brought them back to the wilderness.

So, after the chief had protested for a while against the planting of the cross, Cartier bade the sailors wave a hatchet in the air.

"Come nearer," the sailors called to the chief. "We would like to trade this hatchet for that old bearskin you are wearing."

At first the chief hesitated. Then, in his eagerness for the

24

hatchet, he approached the ships. When the hatchet was almost within his grasp, the sailors seized the canoe and forced the Indians to board Cartier's vessel.

The Indians were at Cartier's mercy, but he treated them kindly and gave them a feast.

"Eat, drink, and be merry," he said to the chief. "We are not going to harm you. We have planted the cross simply as a landmark. In the near future we shall return and bring you iron goods and other gifts. We should also like to take two of your sons to France. If you permit this, we shall return later and bring them to this same harbor."

Then Cartier turned to two of the chief's young sons, who were named Taignoagny and Dom Agaya. He gave each of them a French shirt trimmed with ribbons and a bright red cap and a shining necklace. Taignoagny and Dom Agaya were delighted and with a little help they donned their fine new raiment. Then they told Cartier that they would like to accompany him to France, and their father consented to their going.

Cartier gave the chief two hatchets and a knife. Similar gifts were made to the chief's brother and remaining son, and the three Indians went ashore. In the afternoon twenty-five tribesmen paddled to the ships with fish for Taignoagny and Dom Agaya. By means of signs the tribesmen promised Cartier that they would not tear down the cross which stood on the headland of Cape Gaspé and which was decorated with the fleur-de-lis of France.

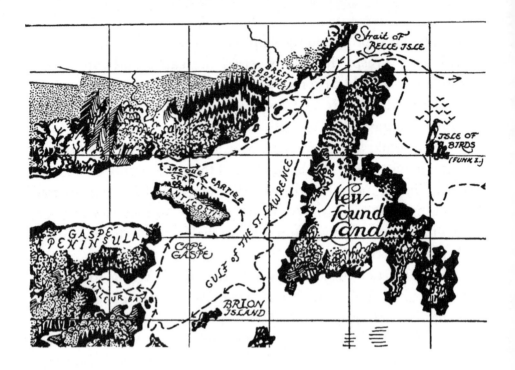

THE RETURN TO ST. MALO

Cartier left Gaspé Peninsula on the twenty-fifth of July, the day after he took the two Indian brothers aboard his ships. Immediately he headed toward land sighted in the northwest. This land is now called Anticosti Island. In sailing to Anticosti from Gaspé Cartier slipped unsuspectingly across the lower arm of the St. Lawrence River at its junction with the Gulf.

His failure to pause and explore the southern arm of the St. Lawrence has puzzled the experts. Up to this point he had probed every promising indentation in the coastline for an outlet to the China Sea. Why did he overlook an arm of a great river that led toward the west? The simplest explanation is that he was in a hurry. His time in North America was running out. By the terms of his commission he must return to France within the year.

26

Yet when Cartier reached the southeast headland of Anticosti Island he did pause to examine a stretch of water he could not resist. This was the upper arm of the St. Lawrence River which flows between Anticosti Island and the mainland of Canada.

Cartier worked his way westward along the north coast of Anticosti. Finally he reached a strait, now called Jacques Cartier Strait, and entered it, although the wind blew heavily against him. When the wind became too strong, he manned a longboat. Thirteen sailors rowed with all their might. They struck a rock, jumped from the longboat, pushed her afloat, and continued westward until they reached a cape (North Point) almost at the northwest tip of Anticosti. Ahead lay an expanse of water that stretched into the west as far as the eye could reach. It looked like a sea. Maybe at last Cartier had found the sea that would take him to China.

Cartier was tempted to spend a few more days exploring his discovery. But he weighed the risks, and they were great indeed. Summer was passing, and the winds at any time might change. And if they changed, he and his men might be held prisoners in this huge wilderness throughout the winter. He had not brought enough provisions to last so long. Nor had he hired his men for such a stay. Perhaps it might be wiser to turn homeward and come back here the following year. Out of consideration for his crew (a consideration rarely found among the bold explorers of the day) Cartier asked his officers and sailors to decide. They voted to return to France.

Jacques Cartier pointed his two small ships toward home and sailed along the Labrador coast for more than four hundred miles. On the fifteenth of August, in the little harbor of Blanc Sablon, near the Strait of Belle Isle, he held religious services to celebrate the feast day of the Assumption. Then he passed through the Strait to the Atlantic. Favorable winds accompanied

him until, in mid-ocean, there arose a storm that raged three days and nights. Cartier felt that only by the grace of God did the two ships ride through the storm.

On the fifth of September 1534, the men in Cartier's expedition saw a small speck in the distance. It was their island seaport of St. Malo. Gradually there loomed into sight the tall spires of the cathedral and the square towers of the old palace and the granite houses that stood huddled close together on the crooked streets. That day every man who had set sail with Cartier reached home safely.

Remarkable stories must have been told that night when the sailors were snug in their houses. It was good to be dressed again in dry, warm clothes and to sit on a chair and have a candle flickering softly at one's elbow. And then, a glass of Breton wine loosened one's tongue and helped to lend magic touches to one's stories. Sitting at home and spinning a yarn was the cream of the voyage, especially if there were children listening.

Perhaps one sailor insisted that in the wild Strait of Belle Isle he had heard fiends howling about the mastheads of his ship; another, that off Labrador he had glimpsed the Bishop of the Sea. (This renowned character of medieval legend was often sighted in regions frequented by seals. Probably the smooth, glistening head, the high, broad fins, and the tapering body of

28

the seal became, through a twist of the imagination, the shaven head, the surplice, and the robes of the elusive Bishop.)

As for the whale, sailors could not let the creature alone. They made him spout fire instead of water and constantly changed his shape and size. They turned him into a monster big enough to swallow a ship, an iceberg, a mouthful of the Atlantic Ocean and parts of Labrador, until the whale's belly looked like a crazy map of the polar regions.

But Jacques Cartier was not concerned with these travels of the imagination. He was impatient with the fabulous world and its phantom maps; he cared only for charts drawn accurately on paper, according to the true findings of a voyage. His circuit of the Gulf of St. Lawrence—the first circuit ever to be recorded by a European navigator—had contributed greatly to man's knowledge of the region west of Newfoundland. Cartier was now eager to return as soon as possible to explore "the unknown sea" which he had discovered beyond the Gulf and which he hoped would prove to be the waterway to China.

The Bishop of the Sea

THE SECOND VOYAGE

THE SECOND VOYAGE

READY TO SAIL AGAIN

Jacques Cartier had not found gold on any of the shores or the islands of the Gulf of St. Lawrence, and the Indians he had met there seemed to be poor, wandering tribes possessing nothing more valuable than birchbark canoes. The King was disappointed in this. But the "unknown sea" which Cartier had discovered beyond Anticosti Island gave such promise of leading westward to China that King Francis agreed to send him on a second voyage to North America. On the thirty-first of October 1534, Brion-Chabot, Admiral of France, signed the Royal Commission instructing Captain Cartier to press forward with his explorations—and to "convert" the Indians.

The conversion of the Indians was an idea which appealed strongly to King Francis. He had listened with interest to Cartier's report that the Indians by the Gulf of St. Lawrence, especially those at Chaleur Bay, could undoubtedly be persuaded to embrace the Catholic faith. This was an opportunity which the King could not afford to miss at a time when many Frenchmen were deserting the Catholic Church to become Protestants.

For centuries France, like the other countries in west Europe, had been a Catholic nation under the spiritual leadership of the Pope at Rome. People did not begin to question the authority of the Catholic Church until the sixteenth century, which was Cartier's century and, in all respects, a period of new ideas. New continents had been discovered, and sea captains had navigated so far from home that they saw stars in the sky which could not be seen from Europe. All these discoveries stimulated men to think along new lines, sometimes rightly and sometimes wrongly, until at last a few people, and then more and more people, protested—and that is why they were called Protestants—that Catholicism was not the best form of Christian worship.

About the time of Cartier's first voyage to North America the number of Protestants in France was increasing to an alarming degree. In October, the month after his return to St. Malo, the Protestants nailed posters in the streets of Paris and other French towns. These posters proclaimed that the Catholic Mass was a pagan celebration and that the statues of the Catholic saints were no better than heathen idols. Many sacred images were smashed to bits as terror spread through France.

King Francis was at a loss to find a solution for the crisis. Political reasons obliged him to let the Protestants keep their new religious beliefs, for a while at least. On the other hand, he did not wish the strength of the Catholic Church to be weakened and he dared not risk the anger of the Pope. Suddenly it occurred to Francis that the Pope might overlook the growth of Protestantism in France if new members could be won in North America for the Catholic Church.

Jacques Cartier seemed to be the ideal person to send overseas on such a mission, for he was a Breton, and Brittany, of all the French provinces, had shut her doors the most firmly against Protestantism. Cartier, in other words, was a devout Catholic, and though he was only a sea captain, he could help prepare the minds of the Indians to accept the Catholic faith at a later date when priests might be sent from France.

But the merchants of St. Malo opposed Cartier's second voyage to North America, just as they had opposed his first. Again they prevented him from getting men and ships which they themselves might need. Cartier was obliged to appeal to Brion-Chabot, Admiral of France, who came to his aid by granting him first choice in ships and a crew.

Cartier obtained three good ships. The largest, the *Grande Hermine*, would be his flagship. She was of one hundred and twenty tons' burden—twice the tonnage of either of the ships used on the first voyage. Next in size came the *Petite Hermine*, of sixty tons, while the third and smallest, the *Emerillon*, was of only forty tons. But the *Emerillon*, a slender galleon, made up in speed and gracefulness for what she lacked in size.

The ships would carry provisions to last fifteen months, and a crew of about one hundred sailors. Cartier also enlisted some extra hands, including carpenters, an apothecary, and a barber surgeon. Hope of discovering the Northwest Passage to China induced several gentlemen of good birth to join the venture.

St. Nicholas, a patron saint of sailors

THE ST. LAWRENCE RIVER

On the sixteenth of May 1535, Captain Jacques Cartier and his men received the bishop's blessing in the cathedral of St. Malo. On the nineteenth of May, feast day of St. Yves, the patron saint of Breton sailors, they boarded their ships. Among those embarking were the Indian brothers, Taignoagny and Dom Agaya, whom Cartier had brought from Canada. Of their stay in France we know only that they had been well treated. They themselves declared so at a later date.

The expedition set sail with favorable winds, but presently a storm arose which swept the three ships far apart from one another. Not until the twenty-sixth of July did they come together at their rendezvous, which was Blanc Sablon Harbor, just west of the Strait of Belle Isle.

From Blanc Sablon, Cartier led his expedition westward along the Labrador coast as far as Bonne Esperance. Then, instead of turning south to circle the Gulf of St. Lawrence, as he had done the previous year, he headed straight across the north section of the Gulf toward his objective: Anticosti Island and the "unknown sea" beyond it.

This course took him along a part of the Labrador coast which is made perilous by thousands of small islands and innumerable shoals and hidden rocks. Cartier stopped frequently to take soundings which he recorded in his logbook, together with other data of interest to navigators, since this might become a much-used route if he discovered the Northwest Passage to China.

Cartier reached Anticosti Island in the early days of August. But heavy storms in the channel between Anticosti and the mainland kept him back from his "unknown sea" that lay beyond the island. He and his men spent the tenth of the month at a bay on the mainland. As the day happened to be the feast day of St. Lawrence, Cartier named the bay in honor of this saint who had once been archdeacon of Rome and whose festival was celebrated with great love throughout Brittany.

As soon as the winds abated, the three ships resumed their westward course. With pennants flying they passed the northwest tip of Anticosti and entered the "unknown sea" which looked as bright and promising as ever. Indeed, its salty waters and regular tides gave every indication of its being a sea—the long-sought sea over which a ship might sail to China.

Now it happened that Cartier's two Indian passengers, Taignoagny and Dom Agaya, recognized this region. And since they had learned a little French in Europe, they could talk with Cartier and understand his questions. When he asked them if this were a sea, they shook their heads.

"It is not a sea," they said. "It is a river. Farther up it grows narrower and the waters become fresh. You can go so far up it that we have never heard of anyone coming to its source."

A river, instead of a sea! A river so long that no Indian had ever reached its source! Then the world must be bigger than anyone had dreamed, and China tremendously far away. China was still Cartier's goal, and reach it he would if any man could. But right now this river that lay in the way—this mighty river he had discovered—absorbed his attention.

Oddly enough, Cartier never gave the river a European name. Years later it became known as the St. Lawrence, the name having come from the little bay that had been baptized on the tenth

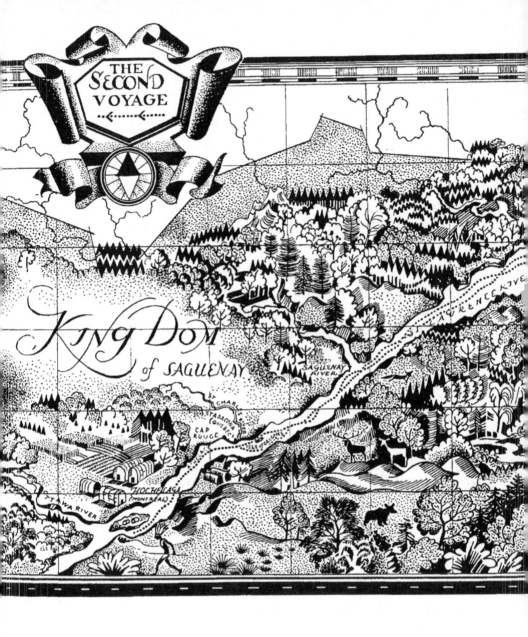

KINGDOM of SAGUENAY

of August. But Cartier himself, in writing of the river, calls it the
River of Hochelaga or the River of Canada, both of them Indian

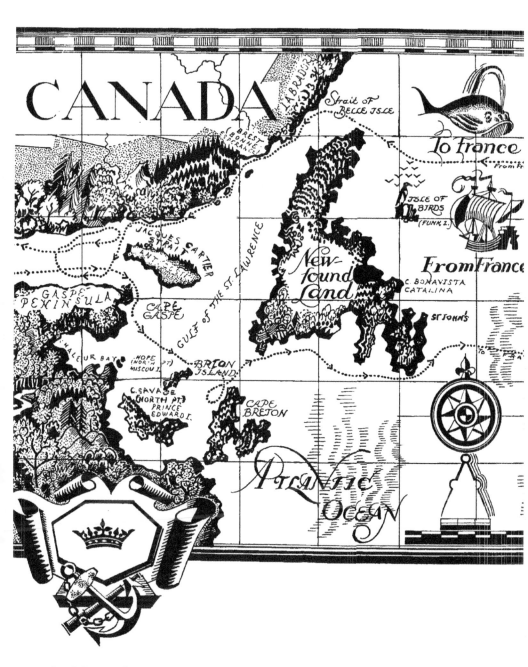

words. More often he calls it simply the River, as if no special
name were needed by a river of such power and majesty.

THE VOYAGE TO STADACONA
(Quebec)

When Cartier realized that he had discovered a great river, he decided to spend a few more days exploring its mouth. So he sailed southward to Gaspé Peninsula, and by doing this he learned that the waters between Anticosti Island and Gaspé form the lower arm of the St. Lawrence. And he learned, too, of the tremendous width of the River's mouth—a maximum of about eighty miles.

Nature on all sides, both on land and in the waters, matched the huge scale of the River. Gaspé Peninsula had its rugged cliffs and towering forests, while in the waters off Gaspé there were so many whales that, in Cartier's own words, "they surpassed all experience."

From Gaspé Cartier returned to the north shore of the St. Lawrence and examined a stretch of coastline he had not yet explored. Then he headed westward up the River.

There are scholars today who claim that long, long before Jacques Cartier was born Viking and Basque sailors had been on the St. Lawrence. Not everyone agrees to this. But of one thing we may be sure: by Cartier's time all records of any early voyages to these parts had disappeared. To Jacques Cartier goes the credit of discovering the River for white men of the modern world.

The joy of discovery, of seeing curiosities and wonders for the first time with fresh eyes, colored Cartier's voyage up the River. He and his hundred sailors and the gentlemen who had come

40

along to share his adventures were quite unprepared for the beauty of what they saw.

First, there was the tremendous spectacle which Nature herself provided. Here was a vast wilderness, a primeval stage upon which there seemed to be no human actors except the Frenchmen aboard Jacques Cartier's three ships. But the huge forests that stretched back from the River abounded in wild life, and so did the River.

Salmon, eels, and lampreys in the salt waters of the River, elk, deer, and moose in the gigantic woods—these were among the inhabitants of the wilderness Jacques Cartier was entering. Some of the creatures were familiar to Europeans, while others were strange and unknown. When they were strange, Cartier described them in his logbook as best he could. Here are his notes on the beluga, or white whale:

We became acquainted with a kind of fish which has not been seen or heard of in man's memory. These fish are about as large as porpoises, but without fins, and are made about the body and head like a greyhound, as white as snow and without a spot. There are many of them living in the River between the salt and fresh water. The natives call them *adothuys* and say that they are very good to eat.

The first white whales had been encountered near the mouth of the Saguenay River, which cuts through the north shore of the St. Lawrence. It is here that the waters of the St. Lawrence begin to lose their saltiness, though the influence of the ocean tides may still be felt.

Cartier's arrival at the mouth of the Saguenay ended one phase of his voyage, for the human inhabitants of the wilderness began to emerge on the scene. As his ships neared the mouth of the Saguenay, four canoes filled with Indians could be seen in the distance. The Indians, who had been fishing quietly, would

41

have fled in terror as the three ships loomed into sight, but Cartier's two Indian passengers, Taignoagny and Dom Agaya, called out in their native language to the fishermen, "Be not afraid." Finally some of the canoes drew near and their occupants came aboard the ships for a brief visit.

As Cartier proceeded up the St. Lawrence, Taignoagny and Dom Agaya told him about the territory through which he was passing. They said that the land on the north shore of the St. Lawrence was divided into three great tribal hunting grounds, which Cartier called "kingdoms."

The first kingdom was known as the Kingdom of Saguenay. From the Kingdom of Saguenay came the copper used by the tribe to which Taignoagny and Dom Agaya belonged. They themselves inhabited the middle kingdom, which they called Canada, an Indian word for "town." Far, far up the River was the third and most important kingdom. It was called Hochelaga, an Indian word meaning "beaver dam," or "place where the river is obstructed." Modern students of the Indian race have identified the Indians of all three kingdoms as Huron-Iroquois.

Cartier was now approaching the middle kingdom, the one known as Canada, where Taignoagny and Dom Agaya lived. The River was growing narrower and narrower, and beyond the forests to the north rose the purple peaks of the Laurentian Mountains.

In early September Cartier passed the isle now called Hare Island, and the verdant isle which he named Isle aux Coudres, meaning Isle of Hazel Trees. Finally he came to a larger island where the wild grapes were so plentiful that his sailors called it Isle of Bacchus, in honor of the Greek god of wine. Cartier

42

himself named it the Isle of Orleans, after his King's young son, the Duke of Orleans. The island has retained the name.

Near the Isle of Orleans Taignoagny and Dom Agaya saw a band of their own tribesmen fishing. The tribesmen were startled by the sight of the two brothers who had sailed away to France. But the brothers called out, "Have no fear. We are alive and well."

Braves, squaws, and children heard the news and hastened to the ships with food and presents. The dancing and rejoicing lasted for many hours. Next day Donnacona, chief of all the surrounding tribes, came down the River with twelve canoes of warriors. He welcomed Cartier with a long speech of friendship. Afterward Cartier entered the chief's canoe and ordered the sailors to bring wine and bread with which to celebrate.

When Cartier had met these tribesmen the previous year they were fishing off Gaspé Peninsula. They now explained to him that their real home was Stadacona, a village about four miles beyond the Isle of Orleans.

Cartier sailed his ships toward Stadacona, and on the fourteenth of September he reached the junction of the St. Lawrence and the little St. Charles River, which flows down from the north. He left his smallest ship, the *Emerillon*, at anchor on the St. Lawrence, for he planned to use her on a voyage of exploration farther up the River. His two large ships were brought into the mouth of the St. Charles and grounded for the winter. A fort would be erected next to them, and the ships and the fort together would serve as the headquarters of the expedition.

In the woods across the St. Charles, near the towering cliffs on which the city of Quebec now stands, lay Stadacona, the village of Chief Donnacona's Indians.

The Atlantic Ocean was more than eight hundred miles away.

INDIAN INTRIGUE

Most of the Stadacona tribe—the Quebec Indians—seemed delighted to have the Frenchmen settling in their neighborhood. Cartier gave them many presents, and the Indians climbed joyfully over his ships. But Taignoagny and Dom Agaya, the two brothers who had gone with him to France, did not join in the merrymaking. Although they had always been friendly toward Cartier, they suddenly began to turn against him. They had

44

promised to guide him up the River to Hochelaga (Montreal). Now they refused to accompany him.

Their change in attitude is hard to account for. Maybe they felt jealous because Cartier wished to go to Montreal, where he would bestow his gifts upon another tribe. But it seems more likely that Taignoagny was a born troublemaker who enjoyed sowing the seeds of discontent, and his true character was beginning to emerge.

Cartier himself was puzzled by Taignoagny. "Why do you refuse to go with me to Hochelaga?" he asked.

"Captain, our chief is angry because you and your sailors carry so many weapons while we carry none."

"You have been in France," replied Cartier. "You know that it is a custom of my people. I am sorry, but I cannot change the custom."

On one occasion, Cartier gave a feast aboard the ships for the leaders of the tribe. Each Indian received a present according to his rank. In the midst of the festivities Taignoagny, the clever one, said to Cartier, "Captain, my chief is vexed because you plan to go to Hochelaga. He says that the River is not worth the risk of the journey. There is nothing there for you. He does not wish me to be your guide."

Cartier replied, "My King wishes me to make the journey. If you are not willing to accompany me, I shall go alone. If you are willing, I shall give you a handsome present—one that will surely please you. You shall be well treated and feasted on the journey. I am going no farther than Hochelaga."

Taignoagny could not be persuaded. On the following day all the tribe—five hundred strong—came singing and dancing down the beach. They drew a large circle in the sand and asked Cartier and his men to step inside. Then Chief Donnacona presented Cartier with three Indian children: two small boys and a girl ten or twelve years old. The tribesmen uttered shouts of peace and friendship, but Taignoagny said, "Captain, the little girl is our chief's own niece, and one of the boys is my brother. We are giving you these children so that you will not go to Hochelaga."

"If that is the reason for your gift," said Cartier, "then the children must be taken back. Nothing can prevent my going."

"Captain," interrupted Dom Agaya, "these children are given through pure affection and as a sign of brotherhood. I myself am willing to accompany you to Hochelaga."

Taignoagny turned angrily to Dom Agaya, and they stood arguing for a long time. Meanwhile Cartier sent men to fetch two swords and two washbasins for Chief Donnacona. The chief was so delighted with these gifts that he shouted to his people to dance, sing, and rejoice. Then he begged the captain to fire the guns on the *Grande Hermine* and the *Petite Hermine*, the two large vessels at the mouth of the St. Charles River. Donnacona said that none of the tribe, except Taignoagny and Dom Agaya, had ever heard a cannon fired.

Cartier granted the request and twelve cannon balls were shot harmlessly across the harbor. The Indians were so terrified by the thunderous noise that they yelled with fright. Taignoagny took advantage of their fear. He pointed to the St. Lawrence where the *Emerillon* rode quietly at her anchor. "Guns on the *Emerillon* were also fired," he said slyly to a friend, "and two of our tribe have just been killed."

Not a word of this was true, but all the Indians believed it and ran like hunted rabbits into the woods.

On the following day Taignoagny appeared on the riverbank with Chief Donnacona and Dom Agaya. "Do you wish to come aboard?" Cartier called out.

"Not now . . . in a little while," answered Taignoagny, who

had thought out an elaborate scheme to frighten Cartier.

The plan consisted of a kind of theatrical performance which began shortly afterward when an Indian canoe came drifting downstream toward the ships. Three fiendish-looking creatures sat in the canoe; their bodies were black and white, their faces black as coal; long horns rose from their foreheads. This was the queerest sight Cartier had yet observed in Canada. At a distance the creatures might perhaps have been taken for devils. But he could see, when they came nearer, that they were merely Indians disguised in dogskins. Then the Indian in the center rose and shouted loudly at Cartier, and as the canoe drifted to the shore, all three of them collapsed as if they had been smitten dead. Chief Donnacona and his warriors bore the canoe and its strange cargo into the woods. The whole tribe followed, and for half an hour Cartier could hear a noisy powwow in the forest.

At last Taignoagny and Dom Agaya emerged woefully. "Jesus, Jesus, Jesus," moaned Taignoagny with hands clasped and eyes rolling skyward.

"Jesus, Maria, Jacques Cartier," groaned Dom Agaya, sending his eyes along the same celestial course.

47

"What is wrong?" asked Cartier.

"Bad news! Bad news!" wailed both the Indians.

"But tell me, friends, what can this bad news be?"

"Captain, our god has sent three devils to predict that there will be ice and snow up the River and that if you venture there, you will perish."

"My friends," retorted Cartier, "your god is a fool and does not know what he is saying. Tell your messengers that our Jesus will keep them safe from cold if they trust in Him."

Taignoagny, the clever one, asked, "Have you spoken to Jesus?"

"I have not, but my priests have, and He predicts fine weather."

Taignoagny and Dom Agaya pretended to be very pleased; they thanked Cartier and went into the woods to fetch the tribe. The tribesmen came with three glad shouts and danced and sang while the brothers had a final word with Cartier. They said, "Unless you leave a hostage with our chief, he will not let us go with you to Hochelaga."

"If you cannot come willingly," said Cartier, "then you may stay at home. I shall not change my plans on your account."

Accordingly, on the following day, the nineteenth of September 1535 Jacques Cartier set sail for Hochelaga (Montreal) without an Indian guide.

THE VOYAGE TO HOCHELAGA
(Montreal)

Part of Cartier's crew had been appointed to remain at Quebec
to build the fort and prepare the winter quarters. Aboard the
Emerillon, which had been chosen for the voyage to Montreal,
were Captain Cartier, all the gentlemen, and fifty sailors.

The St. Lawrence had narrowed at Quebec, but the explorers
soon entered broadening waters and sailed westward on a river
two to three miles wide. The valley through which the River

49

flowed was level and wooded, and the trees were turning to scarlet and gold, for this was the fall of the year.

Of the land itself Cartier said:

Along both shores we saw the most excellent and beautiful land that can be seen, smooth as a pond and covered with the finest trees in the world, and along the River were so many vines laden with grapes that they seemed to have been planted by human hands.

All along the route friendly Indians welcomed the explorers and brought fish to exchange for hatchets, knives, and beads. At Achelacy, by the Richelieu Rapids, the chief of the village boarded the ship, greeted Cartier, and by signs gave warning that navigation became more dangerous farther up the River. Cartier thanked the chief and gave him a feast and European gifts. Then the Chief of Achelacy presented Cartier with a small boy and girl. "These are my son and daughter," said the chief. "They will accompany you on your journey."

The chief wished Cartier to take these children as a token of friendliness and trust, although the boy was only two or three years of age and the girl was nine. "The boy is far too young," said Cartier, "but I am pleased to have the little girl."

When the child embarked aboard the galleon, with its slender prow and billowing sails, she must have felt that she was riding on the back of an enchanted bird.

Forests of superb trees continued to cover the level valley through which the explorers sailed. In his logbook Cartier listed:

Oaks, elms, walnuts, pines, cedars, spruce, ash, boxwood, willows, osiers and what is still better, many vines which were so abundant in grapes that our comrades came back laden with them.

Among the birds he listed:

Cranes, swans, bustards, geese, ducks, larks, pheasants, partridges, blackbirds, thrushes, turtledoves, goldfinches, canaries, linnets, nightingales, sparrows—just as in France.

50

On the twenty-eighth of September Cartier entered a lake (now called Lake St. Peter) on the north shore of the St. Lawrence. There he anchored the *Emerillon* and returned to the St. Lawrence with two longboats, twenty-eight sailors, and several gentlemen. Three days later he reached Montreal, one hundred and sixty-two miles from Quebec and nine hundred and eighty-six miles from the Atlantic.

Cartier could now understand why the Indians called the place Hochelaga, for, as he had learned, the word means not only "beaver dam" but also "place where the river is obstructed." Here there were such swift rapids that Cartier could not cross them even with skillful manning of his longboats.

More than a thousand Indians crowded the banks to welcome Cartier. The tribesmen danced in one ring, the women in another, and the children kept in a circle of their own. After the dancing ceased, the Indians came with great quantities of fish and threw into the longboats loaf after loaf of bread made from Indian corn. When Cartier went ashore, the Indians surrounded him as if he were a god. Squaws brought their babies for him to touch and the rejoicing lasted for more than half an hour. Then he bade the women sit together in a row and he presented them with beads; to the tribesmen he gave knives with shining blades. Although he returned to his boats at suppertime, the Indians did not end their celebration. All night they danced around great bonfires on the shore and called *aguyase, aguyase,* which means *salutation and joy.*

Captain Cartier rose at daybreak, donned his finest armor, and hung a silver whistle around his neck. He organized a group of gentlemen and twenty sailors, the latter carrying trumpets and gilt daggers, and the party started through the meadows with three Indian guides. A headman who had built a bonfire on the path bade the explorers pause to listen to a speech of welcome.

52

For his speech the Indian received two hatchets, two knives, a cross, and a crucifix. Then Cartier and his men continued to walk through field after field of Indian corn until they reached the village.

The village was entirely surrounded by a palisade two lances high and had a single gate which closed with bars. Above the gate and at several other points of the enclosure were galleries equipped with ladders and stocked with stones and rocks for defense. In his logbook Cartier described the enclosure as follows:

There are about fifty houses in the village. Each of these is about fifty or more paces long and twelve or fifteen paces wide, built entirely of wood covered and trimmed with large pieces of bark and strippings from the trees, as broad as tables, and well and artfully seamed, as is their fashion. Within the houses are numerous rooms and chambers and on the ground in the center is a large hearth where they light their fires and live in common. Afterward the men withdraw to their chambers with their wives and children.

And likewise they have garrets aloft in their houses where they put their corn from which they make their bread which they call *carraconny*, and they make this in the following manner. They have wooden mortars, like those for making hemp, and with wooden pestles they pound their corn to powder. Then they lump this into dough and make it into cakes which they place upon hot stones and cover with hot pebbles in place of an oven, and thus cook their bread. They also make many soups of this corn and of beans and peas of which they have quite a supply, and also of large cucumbers and other fruits.

They also have on their houses large vessels like casks where they put their fish, such as eels and others which are smoked during the summer and on which they live in the winter; of these they make a large hoard, as we saw by experience. All their victuals are without any taste of salt. And they sleep on the bark of trees spread upon the ground, with mean coverings of pelts with which they make their garments, such as otters, beavers, martens, foxes, wildcats, deer, stags and many other savage animals; but the majority of them go practically stark naked.

The most precious thing they have in this world is *esnoguy* [wampum] which is white as snow and they take this from cuttle-fish in the river . . . they make it into a kind of rosary bead which they use as we do gold and silver. . . . It has the virtue of stopping nose-bleeds, because we tried it. . . . All these people give themselves to tilling and fishing simply to secure their livelihood, for they place no store upon the goods of this world because they are unacquainted with them and also because they do not budge from their country and are not wanderers like those of Canada [meaning Donnacona's tribe] . . .

Plan of Hochelaga
after the drawing of a Sixteenth Century artist

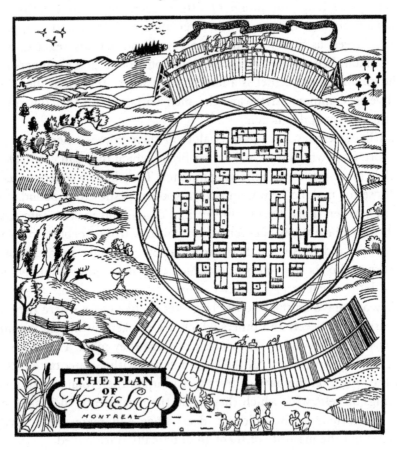

THE VIEW FROM MOUNT ROYAL

The Indians of Montreal still believed that Captain Cartier was a god. They thought that he could drive all harm from them by merely touching them with his hands. When the guides led him to a square in the center of the village, Indian maidens crowded around him and once more the squaws brought their babies for him to touch. Finally the Indian men bade the women withdraw, and Cartier and his party seated themselves on gaily-woven mats while the braves squatted in a circle.

Then the chief was carried in on a large deerskin and placed on a mat by Cartier's side. The chief was an aged man; he wore a crown of porcupine quills painted vivid red; his legs were palsied. He begged the captain to rub those poor old legs, which Cartier did. The chief removed his bright red crown and presented it to Cartier.

The aged and the sick, the lame and the blind pressed around Jacques Cartier to be cured. But he was only a Breton sailor trying in his modest way to bring them word of Christianity. He opened his prayer book and read aloud from the Gospel according to Saint John, which declares that all things were created by God: "Without Him was not anything made that was made." Then Cartier made the sign of the Cross over the sick Indians and prayed aloud to God: "Give them knowledge of our Holy Faith and of our Lord's Passion and grace to regain Christianity and baptism."

To conclude the service Cartier read about the Passion of our

Lord, while all the Indians stood by silently and crossed themselves in imitation of the Christians. Afterward he distributed many European gifts: knives and hatchets for the tribesmen, beads and trinkets for the women. For the children he had brought a supply of images of the *Agnus Dei* or Lamb of God—shining little figures cut from tin in the shape of lambs. Each lamb bore a Cross upon its shoulder and symbolized the Spirit of Christ, whom St. John had called the Lamb of God. Cartier threw handful upon handful of these images into the air, where they were caught by Indian children.

Then the sailors blew their trumpets, and Cartier made a farewell speech. He could not linger with this tribe although the women surrounded him with dishes of beans, soup, bread, and fish and begged him to remain. Winter was approaching, and he must hurry to his fort. But first he wished to get a bird's-eye view of the Montreal region from a mountain which stood a quarter of a league away.

Indian guides led Cartier and his men to the mountain, which he called "Mount Royal." (These two words were afterward combined into the single word Montreal.) When Cartier reached the summit of the mountain, he could see the St. Lawrence flowing on through level lands, with mountain ranges rising to the north and to the south.

He did not know the length of this great River, but he felt sure that, although it might lead toward the Orient, it could not be used by trading vessels because of the rapids at Montreal. Yet he was eager to learn all that he could about the River and the geography of the surrounding country. "How many rapids are there in the River?" he asked his guides.

"Three," replied the Indians.

"After passing the rapids, how far can a canoe go?"

"For three moons."

Then the Indians pointed to the north and indicated the existence of another river, since named the Ottawa. They took Cartier's silver whistle and a gilt dagger from a sailor and remarked, "These metals come from up that river [the Ottawa]. Bad people live there, armed to the teeth. Their armor is made of wood and cords woven and laced together."

"How far away is that country?" asked Cartier.

The question was too difficult for the guides to understand.

Next Cartier showed them a piece of copper. "Does this metal come from that river?" he inquired.

The guides said, "No, that comes from a river to the east," by which they meant the Saguenay.

Cartier vividly remembered the Saguenay's deep, mysterious mouth, which he had passed on his way from Anticosti Island to Quebec. He remembered, too, that the Quebec tribe had told him that its copper came from a region which lay up the river and which was called the Kingdom of Saguenay. It was a kingdom Cartier himself longed to reach someday.

Meanwhile, he must bid farewell to Montreal. As he de-

scended the slopes of the mountain, the Indian guides carried
several of the weary Frenchmen pickaback. When he reached
his longboats, he gave orders to the sailors to push off without
delay. As the longboats proceeded down the St. Lawrence, all
the sorrowing tribe followed him as far as possible along the
shore.

On the fourth of October Cartier entered Lake St. Peter,
where he had left the *Emerillon*. He found all well aboard and
hastened to set sail so that he might reach his headquarters at
Quebec before the River froze.

WINTER AT THE FORT

On the eleventh of October Jacques Cartier arrived at his winter quarters on the banks of the St. Charles River. During his absence the crew had built a strong fort close to the two big ships. The walls had been made by driving logs upright into the earth, and guns were mounted on all sides.

There had been quarrels between the sailors and various Indians who were under the influence of Taignoagny, the mischief-maker, but Cartier's presence helped to re-establish an atmosphere of good feeling. On the twelfth of October Chief Don-

nacona and even Taignoagny and his brother, Dom Agaya, came
with other headmen to welcome the captain and to invite him
to their village.

In Chief Donnacona's wigwam were deerskins to lie upon;
they were trophies of his hunts. There were also scalps of former
enemies, ornamented with wampum beads. This tribe loved war
and would travel hundreds of miles to meet a foe. But as long as
Cartier remained in Canada, the Indians stayed at home and
kept an eye on him. They did this in a friendly way at first and
during the early winter months Cartier paid frequent visits to
Chief Donnacona's dwelling.

Chief *Donnacona*

The chief would sit on one of his fine deerskins and smoke a long pipe of tobacco while he talked. Tobacco smoking was an Indian habit which was new to Cartier. He thought it quite a silly business and said so in his logbook:

They have an herb which they store up in the summer for the winter. They esteem this herb highly and only the men use it, as follows: they dry it in the sun and carry it at their necks in a small animal skin, instead of a bag, with a cornet of wood or stone. Very often they make a powder of this herb and place it in one end of the cornet. Then they put a red-hot coal upon it and suck through the other end and so fill their bodies with smoke that it issues forth from their mouths and nostrils as from a chimney. They say this keeps them healthy and warm. We ourselves tried this smoke but it is so hot that we seemed to have put the powder of pepper in our mouths.

Occasionally Cartier and the Indians talked about religion. They said to him, "We have a god named Cudouagny who sometimes speaks to us and throws dirt in our eyes. When we die we go to the stars and then sink down over the horizon like stars. Then we go into fine green fields filled with trees and flowers and luscious fruit."

"Your Cudouagny is an evil spirit who is tricking you," replied Cartier. "There is only one God Who is in Heaven, and Who gives all, and is the Creator of all things."

One day Chief Donnacona, with Taignoagny and Dom Agaya and all the tribe, came to the fort and said, "Captain, please baptize us with the ceremony which Taignoagny and Dom Agaya saw performed in France."

Cartier, who was not sure that the Indians really believed in Christ, replied, "I have no chrism [consecrated oil] and I cannot baptize without it. On my next trip I shall bring you priests and chrism."

Whenever it was possible Cartier turned his conversation with

61

the Indians to the subject of the Kingdom of Saguenay, which he wished to explore if he came again to Canada. He asked Chief Donnacona many questions about this kingdom.

Donnacona said, "The Saguenay River leads to the Kingdom of Saguenay after one moon's journey from its mouth toward the northwest. But after eight or nine days the Saguenay can be navigated only by small boats. The usual and straight and safest route is by way of the River of Hochelaga [the St. Lawrence] to a place above Hochelaga [Montreal], where there is another river [the Ottawa] which flows down from the Kingdom of Saguenay and enters the River of Hochelaga. From the mouth of the other river [the Ottawa] the journey takes one moon. . . .

"In the Kingdom of Saguenay the natives wear woolen clothes, as you white men do. There are many towns and tribes made up of kindly people who have great quantities of gold and copper. All the region between the Saguenay River as far as Hochelaga [Montreal] and the Kingdom of Saguenay is an island surrounded by rivers and by the River of Hochelaga. Beyond the Kingdom of Saguenay runs the second river [the Ottawa], flowing through two or three large, broad lakes until it reaches a fresh-water sea [Lake Huron]. The people of Saguenay have told us that there is no record of anyone ever having seen the limits of this sea. We ourselves have not been there."

These informing talks with Chief Donnacona came abruptly to an end. One day while the Indians were paying a customary visit to the ships to exchange fish for European wares, Taignoagny and Dom Agaya said, "Brothers, you are fools to be

pleased with such trifles. You think these little things are great, but we who have been to France know better."

Little by little the Indians became dissatisfied. They grew more restless and quarrelsome as time passed and it seemed as if sooner or later they would come to blows with the sailors.

Once the Chief of Achelacy journeyed down the River to pay a visit to his small daughter, who had been with the Frenchmen ever since she accompanied them to Montreal. When her father found that she was well and happy, he permitted her to remain at the fort. But he was much distressed by the state of affairs in the tribe at Quebec. "Captain," he said, "beware of Taignoagny and Dom Agaya and even of Chief Donnacona. These rogues can mean no good."

Cartier summoned his mates and told them about this warning of the Chief of Achelacy. Then he said to them, "Strengthen the fort on all sides with wide, deep ditches and with a gate with a drawbridge and reinforcements of logs set crosswise. Count off fifty men for night guard and sound the trumpets at the change of watch."

Snow fell and the River froze. The Frenchmen muffled themselves thickly against the wind that whipped the cheeks and stung the blood cold beneath the skin. A man from France could only marvel at the Indian children who ran laughing and stark naked over the ice and snow.

64

DEATH IN THE WILDERNESS

Sickness entered the wilderness, stole across the snows of the forest, and over the ice of the River and into the Indian village. Forty members of the tribe, including Dom Agaya, were dying. Taignoagny visited the fort and begged for salt and bread to give his brother. "Very well," said Cartier, "but in return I ask that none of you come near us for fear of spreading the disease."

The sickness came of its own accord. The ditches around the fort and the gate, the drawbridge and the night guard could not hold it back, nor could the trumpets warn of its approach. It came, and no one could fight it because no one knew from which side it would strike, or why it struck, or what it was. One hundred of the one hundred and ten men of the expedition were stricken. Eight men died and fifty more seemed doomed to die.

Cartier was among the lucky ones to escape. We know today that this disease, which we call scurvy, is caused by a lack of fresh vegetables. However, no one in the sixteenth century understood this, and Cartier was completely mystified as he studied the symptoms. He saw that the victims first lost their strength and that afterward their legs became swollen and bloated, with the sinews contracting and blackening to the color of coal. Sometimes a purplish blood blotched the legs before the disease crept upward, mounting to the hips and to the shoulders and spreading down the arms and up the neck. The gums became so rotted that the teeth fell out. And still Cartier was at a loss to find a way of checking the epidemic.

In his despair he fastened a picture of the Virgin Mary to a tree near the fort. On Sunday he held a religious service beneath the tree, and there he sent all the sailors who were well and all who were ill but could still walk. They went stumbling and staggering and singing the psalms of David. Cartier made a vow that if he were permitted to return alive to France, he would make a pilgrimage to the Virgin's shrine at Rocadamour.

On this same day there died a young man in his early twenties;

his name was Philippe Rougemont. In those times the belief prevailed in Europe that the bodies of the dead belonged to God. Only here and there did a rare and intelligent doctor take a corpse and cut it open to study at close range the cause of death. Even at the great French medical center of Montpellier students of anatomy were allowed to dissect only one dead body a year, and it must be the body of a hanged man. But Cartier had the corpse of Philippe Rougemont opened and dissected. The results of the investigation were carefully recorded in the logbook:

We found that his heart was white and withered and surrounded by more than a potful of water colored reddish like dates. His liver was excellent but his lungs were completely blackened and gangrened, and all his blood had been drawn from above his heart, because when we opened him there gushed forth from above his heart a great quantity of black and poisonous blood. He also had spleen near the spine, and about two finger-lengths of his spine were somewhat damaged, as if it had been rubbed on a rough stone. This seen, we opened his thigh, which was very black outside, but inside the flesh was fine enough. That done, we buried him as best we could. God by His Holy Grace forgive his soul and the souls of all our dead. Amen.

Yet the investigation did not suggest a cure for scurvy; more of the men were stricken, and more and more lay dying. It was December, and the snow stood four feet deep in the forest. As no one had strength to dig in the frozen ground, the dead were buried underneath the snow. Of all the company only Cartier and three others escaped the epidemic.

Indians began to lurk about the fort and Cartier feared that if they learned how weak his company had grown, they might think the time favorable for an attack. Therefore he tried his best to give them the impression that life at the fort was running smoothly. Whenever the Indians appeared, he ordered two or three sailors, sick or well, to follow him outside the walls, and there he would pretend to beat his men and to throw sticks at them as if to say, "See here, the rest are working down below the decks. You chaps can't loaf out here." Aboard the ships the feeble men took stones and hammers and faked as loud a sound of caulking as was possible. All this happened while the ships were locked in two fathoms of river ice. Above and below the hatches the ice hung four fingers deep.

Cartier lost all hope of seeing France again. But one day Dom Agaya paid an unexpected visit to the fort. "How is this?" cried Cartier. "Twelve days ago you were desperately ill and here you come as strong and well as any man. What has cured you?"

"A brew made from the leaves of a tree," answered Dom Agaya.

Cartier said guardedly, "Is there one of these trees nearby? I would like to cure one of my sailors, who caught the disease when he visited Donnacona's wigwam."

"I will send you two squaws with some of the branches," said Dom Agaya, who, when he was sick, had received bread and salt from Cartier.

The squaws came with nine or ten branches of a tree which Cartier called the *ameda*, and which was probably a variety of evergreen. The women showed him how to grind the bark and boil it with the leaves. At first the sailors were afraid of the mixture, but finally one or two poor fellows were brave enough to taste it. They felt better immediately, and then all the others fought for a drink. Cartier dosed them every other day and with the dregs he poulticed swollen legs and other diseased parts of the body. The remedy succeeded, and within the next few days a tall tree was consumed.

Cartier remarked in his logbook:

If all the doctors of Louvain and Montpellier had been here with all the drugs of Alexandria, they could not have done as much in a year as this has done in eight days.

He gave thanks to heaven, and added:

God has had pity on us and sent us the knowledge and remedy for our cure.

A DREAM TO
COLONIZE CANADA

By the end of March the snow was melting in the forest and the ice was breaking in the River. Nearly a year had passed since Cartier sailed from France with his commission for a voyage of fifteen months' duration. His provisions now were almost exhausted, and as soon as the River cleared itself of ice, he must return home. Yet he had not found the Northwest Passage, for even if the St. Lawrence did lead eventually to the China Sea, trading vessels could sail no farther than the rapids at Montreal.

All that Cartier had actually discovered was a river and a wilderness. However, his practical mind understood the greatness of this River, which abounded in fish, enriched the soil of Canada, and sustained the mighty forests. In this wilderness lived the elk, the deer, and the moose, king of the forest, the fox, the wolf, the black bear, rabbits, woodchucks, chipmunks, squirrels, and game so plentiful that it was more than enough for the few scattered Indian tribes which inhabited the region. But in France food was scarce and poor people could hardly pay the heavy taxes. Jacques Cartier wished to make the natural resources of the wilderness available to Frenchmen by establishing a colony in Canada.

He dreamed of the day when French pioneers would clear the land and sow French crops in the rich soil, when French cattle would graze in the Canadian meadows, and when along the banks of the St. Lawrence would stand French settlements with farms and water mills and windmills. He did not doubt that the Indians would benefit by contact with civilization and Christianity.

But Cartier realized that it might be difficult to convince King Francis of the advantages to be gained from colonizing the Canadian wilderness, where neither gold nor silver had been found. Probably the King would think enviously of Spain's vast possessions in the southern regions of the New World, where gold and silver were abundant. This was the year 1536, and stories were beginning to drift back to Europe of the golden empire of Peru which Pizarro had just conquered for the Emperor of Spain. Pizarro had shod his horses with Peruvian silver, stood in temples glittering with gold, and received from one Inca war lord a single ransom amounting to nearly eight million dollars.

Perhaps in the Kingdom of Saguenay could be found those treasures of which kings dreamed. Certainly the stories the Indians told of the Kingdom pointed to this, and Cartier could repeat to King Francis what the Indians had said. But how much more authentic the stories would sound if King Francis could hear them from Chief Donnacona himself.

Cartier decided to take the chief to France, along with half-a-dozen tribesmen whose bronze skin and picturesque looks would help stimulate the King's interest in Canada. But it was obvious that none of the Indians would go willingly to France. Of late the quarrels between the tribesmen and some of the rough sailors had increased in violence. When the time came for Cartier to leave Canada, he would have to seize his Indians by force.

THE CAPTURE OF
CHIEF DONNACONA

One day in early April Dom Agaya came to the fort with news that Chief Donnacona had gone on a hunt. But Cartier wondered if the chief had not really gone to secure reinforcements from another tribe in order to attack the fort. Cartier therefore called his mates together and said, "Strengthen the fort so that if the chief comes with all the army of Canada, he can only stare at us."

On the twenty-first of April Dom Agaya reappeared at the fort; this time he was accompanied by several braves from a tribe unknown to the explorers. Dom Agaya said to Cartier, "Captain, my chief comes back tomorrow. He will bring you deer meat."

On the following day Dom Agaya came to the riverbank near the fort and cried out that Chief Donnacona had returned. Cartier invited Dom Agaya to board the ships, but the Indian remained sullenly on shore—and then vanished into the woods.

Cartier's suspicions were thoroughly aroused and he decided to send two men to the village to find out what was happening. Both men had previously been welcome visitors in the village, but now when they went there, the atmosphere was hostile and the place crowded with powerful warriors from an unknown tribe. When the Frenchmen entered Chief Donnacona's wigwam, they found him lying on a deerskin; he pretended to be too ill to receive them. Next they visited Taignoagny, the mischief-maker. In his wigwam stood fierce-looking warriors, and he wished to get rid of the two Frenchmen as soon as possible. Yet he had a favor to ask.

So the mischief-maker led the two white visitors out of his wigwam and along the path toward the fort. He said to them, "There is something you can do for me. If your captain will do this, he can count on me for anything he asks. There is a chief living in this region who belongs to our tribe. He has done me a great wrong. His name is Agona, and I would like your captain to take him to France. Will you bring me the answer tomorrow?"

After the Frenchmen promised Taignoagny to deliver his message, he accompanied them halfway to the fort and then returned to his village.

When Cartier learned that Quebec was filled with warriors, he realized that, to avoid bloodshed, the Indians whom he wished to take to King Francis must be captured by trickery. Taignoagny and his brother, Dom Agaya, must also be seized so that they could serve as interpreters on the voyage. Cartier was not interested in the petty chief, Agona, whom Taignoagny wanted to send to France. Yet one of the Frenchmen who had brought the message was sent back to the village, where he found Taignoagny and said to him, "The captain promises to do part of what you ask, but first he wants to see you."

"I will come tomorrow and bring Chief Donnacona and Dom Agaya," replied Taignoagny. But for two days not an Indian ventured near the fort.

Meanwhile Cartier began to make active preparations for the homeward journey. His crew had been so reduced by scurvy that he could not man his second vessel, the *Petite Hermine*. He dismantled and abandoned her and let some friendly Indians from a neighboring tribe dig the precious iron nails from her hull. When Chief Donnacona's tribesmen saw this, they paddled in great haste to the fort. Taignoagny and Dom Agaya stood talking together on the shore for half an hour before they would board the vessels. Then Taignoagny, who was still plotting against his enemy, Agona, said to Cartier, "Captain, please take Agona back to France."

"I cannot take Agona," replied Cartier. "My King has forbidden me to take any grown Indian, man or woman. Only two or three boys can go with me to learn the language. If you wish I will take Agona and leave him in Newfoundland."

"Ai! Ai! Tomorrow I shall bring Chief Donnacona and all our tribe to you," said Taignoagny. And he went away rejoicing.

Cartier had not been forbidden to take grown Indians to France. He told this lie because he wished to put the Indians off their guard so that he might seize them with as little violence as possible and thus avoid the bloodshed that had cast a blot on most European explorations of the New World.

From the day when Columbus discovered the Americas, the Indians seemed to have been doomed to yield sooner or later to the white race. But the primitive law of nature which decrees that the weak shall yield to the strong often gives the strong a chance to be unnecessarily arrogant and cruel. Compared to the average explorer of those days, Jacques Cartier was remarkably kind in his treatment of the Indians. Even on this occasion, when he felt that he was justified in lying to them and in forcing some of them to accompany him to France, he did hope to bring his captives back safe and sound to Canada, after they had told the King about the riches in Saguenay.

On the morning of the third of May, the festival of the Holy

74

Cross, the sailors planted an enormous cross of possession near the fort. The shaft rose thirty-five feet in the air, and on the crossbar were the words:

LONG LIVE FRANCIS THE FIRST, BY
GOD'S GRACE, KING OF FRANCE.

At two o'clock in the afternoon Chief Donnacona and the brothers, Taignoagny and Dom Agaya, came with other headmen toward the fort. Cartier, who was on the *Grande Hermine,* went down to greet them. Although the chief seemed in a friendly mood, his eyes roamed anxiously toward the woods. Cartier invited the Indians to come aboard, as was the custom. But Dom Agaya took Cartier aside and said, "Taignoagny has warned our chief not to board your ships under any circumstance."

Other tribesmen came and outside the ramparts they built a fire for Chief Donnacona, who had also been warned not to enter the fort. Finally Cartier persuaded the chief to come inside, and Taignoagny, Dom Agaya, and many of the tribe went in with Donnacona. Suddenly Cartier ordered his sailors to capture Donnacona, Taignoagny, Dom Agaya, and six headmen. The other Indians were driven off, and as they fled, Cartier thought with a touch of disgust, "They go like sheep before a wolf, some across the river, others into the forest; each man seeks his private safety."

But the Indians had not abandoned their chief. At dusk they gathered on the opposite shore and stood there all night long, howling for Donnacona. They wailed far into the morning and by afternoon more than a thousand of them stood crying piteously. Finally, at Cartier's request, Chief Donnacona appeared

on deck and reassured them. "I am going with the captain to see his King," cried Donnacona, who had been soothed by promises from Cartier. "I shall be given a fine present and in ten or twelve moons I shall return."

"Ho! Ho! Ho!" yelled the Indians in joy. They came now to the ships and presented Cartier with twenty-four strings of precious wampum. He thanked the Indians and gave them European gifts. To Donnacona he gave two brass kettles, eight hatchets, many knives, and beads. The chief seemed pleased and sent the presents to his wives and children.

On the following day four squaws boarded the ships with corn, fresh meat, and other provisions for the captives. Cartier again promised that the chief would be brought back within a year. "Captain," said the squaws, each offering him a string of wampum, "the day our chief returns, and the other Indians with him, our tribe will give you many presents."

Donnacona chose Agona, the petty chieftain, as temporary head of the tribe. On the sixth of May 1536 Jacques Cartier weighed anchor. In addition to his nine captives there was one other Indian aboard the ships: the little daughter of the Chief of Achelacy. She had accompanied the Frenchmen to Montreal, visited them at their fort near Quebec, and now was permitted by her father to cross the seas with Captain Cartier.

Cartier lost no time in heading down the St. Lawrence River toward its fork at Anticosti Island. He knew that if he sailed through the strait that separated the north coast of Anticosti and the Canadian mainland, he could then navigate along the coast of Labrador to the Atlantic. That was the long route by which he had come to Canada. Now he preferred to find a shorter way home.

Previously, while making his first exploration of the Gulf of St. Lawrence, Cartier had noticed that the tides at Brion Island

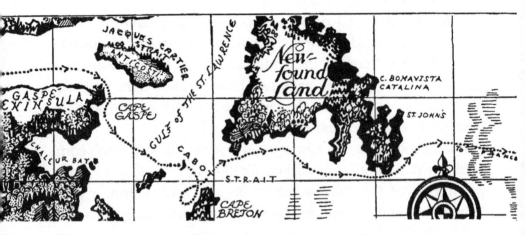

ran northwest, southeast. This observation had made him suspect that possibly a short passage to the Atlantic existed along the south coast of Newfoundland. So this time he entered the Gulf through the southern arm of the St. Lawrence River, between the south coast of Anticosti and the Gaspé Peninsula.

It was a new route for him but not a difficult one, and he was soon in a familiar region. He continued to navigate southeastward through the Gulf until he discovered a strait, the present Cabot Strait, lying between Cape Breton and the south coast of Newfoundland. He found, to his joy, that Cabot Strait led him quickly to the Atlantic. On the nineteenth of June he began the ocean voyage. Good winds and a favorable sea permitted him to reach St. Malo on the sixth of July 1536.

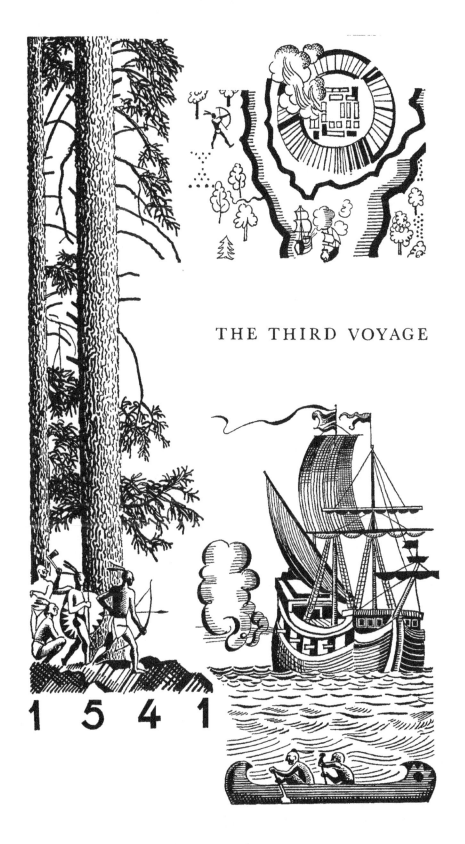

THE THIRD VOYAGE

1 5 4 1

THE THIRD VOYAGE

YEARS OF WAITING

None of the ten Indians brought by Cartier to France in 1536 saw Canada again. The King was so weighed down by troubles that he had no time to listen to Cartier's plan to colonize. In that same year the King's eldest son, the Dauphin, died suddenly—from poisoning, most people thought—and the arch-enemy, the Emperor of Spain, came with his army to invade the south of France. Furthermore, it was disastrous for Cartier that his "friend at Court," Brion-Chabot, Admiral of France and favorite minister of King Francis, had turned traitor to his country and sold himself to the enemy, Portugal.

The ten Indians, who were staying in St. Malo, were well lodged and treated kindly. An old church notice has been found which tells us that three of them were baptized. One took the name of Charles, another chose the King's own name, Francis, the third . . . but here a corner of the paper on which the notice was recorded has been torn off. The name of the third Indian will never be known.

At last, in 1538, peace between France and Spain was declared by the Treaty of Nice. Then Cartier presented his plans to the new royal advisor, Constable de Montmorency, who brought them to King Francis' attention. In September Francis ordered his treasurer to pay Captain Cartier and his men salaries long overdue; the captain was also reimbursed for the money he had paid to lodge the Indians.

Chief Donnacona, who was taken to court, thrilled King Francis with glowing tales of the Kingdom of Saguenay. Probably Francis saw the other captive Indians and admired their picturesque looks. But they, themselves, could not grow used to civilization; they found it difficult to live in houses and to ward off the germs that thrive in towns and cities. One by one the Indian men fell ill and before Cartier had the chance to take them back to Canada, they died. Only the little girl, the daughter of the Chief of Achelacy, survived. She had come to France when she was ten or eleven years of age—young enough to become accustomed to her new surroundings.

In September 1538 Cartier drew up an outline of a simple plan for establishing a settlement in Canada. In this outline, which he sent in the form of a memorandum to the royal palace, he asked for six large ships, two small boats, and one hundred and twenty sailors, as well as soldiers to maintain order, priests to spread Catholicism, carpenters and masons, tailors, blacksmiths, apothecaries to study the medicinal qualities of Canadian herbs, goldsmiths to examine ores, in fact all the workmen and technicians needed to establish the colony on a sound basis.

But the King, though eager for the riches of Saguenay, could not decide to send a colonial expedition immediately.

82

KINGS AND SPIES

The kings of Portugal and Spain were exceedingly annoyed by
the rumor that France intended to establish a colony in Canada.
They believed that they alone possessed the right of conquest in
the Americas, for in 1493, the year after Columbus found the
New World, the Pope at Rome had declared that all the heathen
lands discovered, and to be discovered, should belong to Spain
and Portugal. The Pope said that one hundred and twenty
leagues west of the Azores a kind of imaginary boundary line
should be drawn from Pole to Pole. Territory in the East, beyond
this line, should become the property of the Portuguese; territory

84

in the West, that of the Spaniards. Roughly speaking, for no one could accurately measure longitude, this law gave the Orient to Portugal and the Americas to Spain.

Afterward, except for a colony in Brazil, Portugal had acquired her territory in the Orient. By navigating the ten-thousand-mile route around Africa to Asia, she had managed to acquire footholds in India, Borneo, the Spice Islands, and eventually in China and Japan. And now Portugal was wondering if the French scheme to colonize Canada did not mean that France had found a quick Northwest Passage which would threaten Portuguese supremacy in the East.

King John of Portugal sent a spy, Lagarto, to France to investigate the matter. Lagarto's task was not too difficult since there were enemies on all sides of Cartier. Even at the French court, among the friends of King Francis, there were men who would sell their honor for a little gold. Lagarto met these traitors and through them he gained entry to the royal palace. He claimed to be an expert pilot and played the role so well that in January 1539 he obtained a private interview with Francis.

"Your Majesty," said Lagarto when he was presented to the King, "I have brought two maps and the astrolabe which belonged to my brother-in-law. I place great value on them; I have never given a copy of the maps to anyone or been willing to sell them."

"Let me see the maps," said Francis, who watched eagerly while Lagarto spread them out.

The two men talked together for more than an hour until Constable de Montmorency, the King's advisor, entered the royal chamber and said, "Your Majesty, with whom are you speaking?"

"With a person well informed in navigation. He has splendid sea charts and an astrolabe. I am delighted with him; he is going to enter my service."

"Your Majesty," said the constable abruptly, "this matter should be examined and discussed in council."

The King was somewhat taken aback, but replied royally, "If that is so, let it be at dessert, after supper."

In spite of his advisor's warning, Francis saw Lagarto several other times. The King was glad to play an indoor game of exploration with this man whose knowledge of the sea was so profound

and whose personal manner was so charming. One day Francis showed the spy two finely colored maps and said, pointing to the St. Lawrence, "Here is the River of Cod. This has been charted at my request. Twice I have sent Jacques Cartier there, and I shall send him a third time."

The game was thrilling for Lagarto. He plied the King with subtle questions and finally learned that, in Jacques Cartier's opinion, the St. Lawrence River did not lead to China, but that by crossing the rapids at Montreal, Cartier did hope to reach Saguenay.

"In the Kingdom of Saguenay," Francis said, "there are abundant mines of gold and silver; men dress and wear shoes as we do, and there is a quantity of clover, nutmeg, and pepper. I shall send six ships with over two hundred men and supplies to last two years. Cartier is to build a fort well up the River. That will be done in the summer and then, because the summers are short and the winters long and extremely cold, he shall set out in the following spring to cross the rapids and find the Kingdom. Two of the ships will be brigantines so that they may be carried overland when the rapids are reached. Saguenay is a wonderful country, for it has animals whose hides are worth ten cruzados each—and men who fly with wings on their arms like bats, although they fly only a little, from the ground to a tree and from the tree to the ground."

"Your Majesty, has Cartier seen those flying men?" inquired Lagarto.

"Donnacona has seen them," replied Francis. "He is the chief of three or four villages. He has told me about the Kingdom of Saguenay. What do you think?"

"Your Majesty, your River lies in the Tropic of Cancer but it is farther north than the distance of the Tropic of Cancer to the equator, and it seems to me that spices and gold could not be found there, although there might be silver."

"In Hungary," argued the King, "there is a mine, or rather there are several mines, of excellent gold, and that country is just as cold—even colder, because it lies farther north of the equator."

"Your Majesty, that is so, but is it not a rare thing and not the general rule?"

"Donnacona has said it is true," replied King Francis. "When he went aboard Cartier's ship, he was questioned and the notary

88

wrote down his answers, and since then Cartier has questioned him many times and Donnacona has never varied in his statements. He even says that he will go with all his people, friends, and relatives to help us cross the rapids with the brigantines and find the clover, nutmeg, and pepper plants."

"Your Majesty, what if Donnacona should be like the one who tempted Christ by saying, *Haec omnia tibi dabo* [all these things shall I give to thee]—in order to return to his own country?"

King Francis laughed; he was in a merry mood and there was very little that he did not tell Lagarto about the colonial plans. "Ah, Your Majesty is a Fountain of Knowledge!" cried Lagarto when the King had finished.

Then the spy dispatched a long report on these proceedings to King John of Portugal. "What the French King wants to do in this colonial business is enough to make men marvel," said Lagarto in his letter to King John.

But it was enough for King John to know that Cartier had not found the Northwest Passage to China.

Spain had much more reason to worry about French colonial plans, as her possessions lay in the southern part of the New World and were slowly creeping northward. Charles the Fifth, the Spanish Emperor, did not wish the French to gain a foothold across the Atlantic, no matter how far north.

The position of King Francis in this matter was extremely awkward. Since the Treaty of Nice in 1538 he had been trying to be friendly toward Emperor Charles. Francis had even given Charles permission to cut across France on his way to suppress a revolt in Flanders. In the fall of 1539 the Emperor planned to take advantage of this offer. Not only would he travel across France but he would also pay a visit to "dear Francis." It seemed to the King that it would be more tactful to put the Canadian project aside during this year.

The Emperor came, and he and Francis rode together to the forest of Fontainebleau to hunt. They picnicked under purple canopies spread beneath great oak trees almost as old as the land. The forest was King Francis' pride. Thousands of men worked in his stables, and wells had been dug in the woods so that wild animals might drink and thrive to furnish sport for the royal hunt. The old hunting lodge of his ancestors had been torn down and in its place stood a magnificent palace where the King held his brilliant court. Amidst all the festivities at Fontainebleau the King forgot the sea captain of St. Malo.

90

It was not until the seventeenth of October 1540, long after the Emperor of Spain had gone from France, that Jacques Cartier received a definite commission to make ready for the colonial expedition.

In this commission the King expressed his *full confidence in the person of Jacques Cartier, and in his judgment, competency, loyalty, integrity, courage, great industry, and experience,* and said that as a reward for past services Cartier should be given the *Emerillon.* She was the little galleon that had made the memorable journey up the St. Lawrence from Quebec to Montreal.

In November Spanish spies were ordered to the ports of France to learn the latest developments in Cartier's plans. Secret agents sped up and down the coast of France, and from Spain and Portugal to Africa, where Charles the Fifth had gone on state affairs. Every rumor seemed precious. Whether it was true or false, it was dispatched to Emperor Charles, who wrote, also in November, to his Cardinal at Toledo: "Some people say that Cartier will set out with twelve vessels, others say eighteen, and still others, twenty vessels. And my Ambassador, when he asked the Constable of France to rectify the matter, was told that this Cartier had gone to explore regions not belonging to us or to the Most Serene King of Portugal, and that any one may go to unpopulated lands, even though discovered."

This letter continued with instructions for the Spaniards to prepare a fleet and concluded by saying: "If our fleet encounters the vessels of the said Jacques or any other Frenchmen with an expedition bound for the Indies, let our ships fight and destroy the Frenchmen since we know their intentions, and let all their men be taken from their vessels and cast into the ocean, and let no one be spared because this is necessary as a warning against similar expeditions."

Spain tried several times to secure the help of Portugal against the French colonial undertaking. But John of Portugal knew that his father had previously sent two fleets to Newfoundland and had lost them and he himself had lost two expeditions there. As far as he was concerned France might go where she wished on the cold northern waters. "The Ocean is so wide," said John, "that never could we form a fleet to keep those Frenchmen from going to explore. If a thousand vessels were armed, they could not keep the Frenchmen from sailing where they wish."

Emperor Charles protested once more to the French King through the Spanish Ambassador in France. The Ambassador told King Francis that the colonial scheme was contrary to both the Treaty of Nice and the Pope's old law which gave the sole ownership of the Americas to Portugal and Spain. King Francis answered, "The sun shines for me as it shines for others. I should like to see the clause in Adam's testament that prevents me from sharing the world."

THE COLONIAL EXPEDITION

Those alarming rumors about a giant fleet for Cartier were false. Five ships were all that he planned to take, and once again the merchants of St. Malo were preventing him from getting sailors. In December 1540 King Francis was obliged to write to a government official in Brittany to inquire why the people of the Breton seaports were hindering *"dear and beloved Jacques Cartier."* Suddenly at this point Francis, spoiled sovereign that he was, grew weary and lost interest in the project which had been so long delayed.

Among the royal courtiers there was a lord, a dashing man whose name was Jean-François de La Rocque de Roberval. He borrowed Cartier's plan and decked it out afresh in gay, imperial colors which caught the fancy of the King. In January 1541 Francis appointed Roberval to the post of commander in chief of the expedition, with the title of Lieutenant-General of the countries of Canada, Hochelaga, and Saguenay, and with the right to conquer the distant lands either by peace or by force and to build forts and castles on any territory not occupied by Spain or Portugal. Captain Cartier was reduced to a subordinate position under this inefficient lord who had never had experience at sea, who could neither handle men nor organize an enterprise, and who had no notion of what a wilderness was like.

Roberval looked upon the establishment of the colony as a purely business venture. He planned to divide the territory into fiefs and to share the profits with the King. The vessels to be used were the five that Cartier was equipping at St. Malo, and he was instructed to continue with his preparations. Roberval agreed to take charge of supplying the guns and ammunition, but his credit was so bad that in spite of his titles and innumerable castles, he could not raise sufficient money to proceed with his part of the work. By the first of May, Roberval's war supplies had not yet been delivered in St. Malo. King Francis fretted at the delay; would the expedition never set sail?

But Jacques Cartier was ready; he was blind to obstacles and had the unbreakable will that has always sent great sea captains on their journeys over the world. His five ships lay waiting at St. Malo, among them the *Grande Hermine* and the *Emerillon*. A group of noblemen and gentlemen who had decided to accompany him were at hand, and these included men of his own family whom he could trust. In his service were twenty master pilots, one hundred and twenty sailors dressed in the King's colors of

94

Lord de Roberval

black and white, one hundred and fifty mechanics and soldiers, six priests, two apothecaries, and twenty plowmen with carts and implements. Like a careful farmer Cartier was planning to graft a little of the Old World upon the New. His ships were stocked with barnyard animals: four bulls, ten pigs, twenty horses, twenty cows, and one hundred goats.

But it had been difficult to obtain volunteers for the colony. An honest freeman, however poor he might be, would not dream of leaving his native land for a strange wilderness. Therefore the colonists had to be recruited from the prisons. Murderers, thieves, and prisoners of all kinds, provided they were not Protestants, were given a chance to start life again in Canada. These men, who reached St. Malo in chains, were not of the stuff that makes good pioneers.

King Francis ordered Cartier to set sail, with the understanding that Lord de Roberval should follow shortly afterward with reinforcements of men and supplies. Roberval went to St. Malo and reviewed Cartier's fleet. On the twenty-third of May 1541 Jacques Cartier weighed anchor and started on his third official voyage across the Atlantic Ocean. Three months later, after terrific storms, during which the animals aboard almost died of thirst, his five vessels met near Quebec.

The fleet with which Spain had hoped to fight all Frenchmen bound for the Americas was never equipped. One Spanish vessel only was dispatched to Newfoundland, but by then Jacques Cartier had disappeared up the St. Lawrence River.

Back on the coast of Normandy, in northern France, Jean-François de La Rocque de Roberval, commander in chief of the colonial enterprise, became a rascally pirate, plundering ships for the money which he still needed to follow Cartier.

IN SEARCH OF THE
KINGDOM OF SAGUENAY

Five years had elapsed since the fateful day when Cartier seized
Chief Donnacona and the eight braves by trickery. All that time
the tribe had waited for the chief and the other captives to return. Cartier had promised to bring them back within twelve
moons. But five times twelve moons had passed, and when at last
the captain's ships reached Quebec, none of the captives was
aboard.

Agona, who had been chief of the tribe during Donnacona's
absence, came to the ships to greet the captain. When Agona
asked about the Indians who had gone to France, Cartier, hoping
to protect his own men from the vengeance of the tribe, said,
"Some of those Indians have married and others are living in
France like great lords. But Donnacona is dead; his body rests in
the earth."

98

The tribe grieved for Donnacona, but Agona himself was glad that he could continue to be chief. In his joy he removed his royal headdress and wampum bracelets and handed them to Cartier. But Cartier had no use for an Indian crown; the business of the voyage was pressing him. He invited the chief to a feast on shore, returned the headdress, and sailed a little farther up the St. Lawrence. At its junction with the Cap Rouge River he found a protected site for the colonial settlement. So he anchored three of his ships in the harbor of the Cap Rouge and sent the others back to France to tell King Francis that Roberval had not arrived with the promised reinforcements.

Curiously enough, on the shores of the Cap Rouge River Cartier discovered nuggets which he believed to be gold: "As thick as a man's nail," he called them in his logbook. And on the slopes of a neighboring mountain he found crystal-like stones. "Diamonds!" he cried joyfully. "No man could ever see more beautiful diamonds. When the sun shines on them they glisten as if they were sparkles of fire." The Kingdom of Saguenay, with its vaunted riches, seemed nearer and more attainable than before and Cartier planned a reconnoitering trip to the rapids at Montreal so that, in the following spring, he might lead an expedition over them to the mouth of the Ottawa River.

Cartier did not begin his voyage until the settlement on the Cap Rouge River was well established. The buildings consisted of two forts. One of them, located on the top of a cliff, had a fine tower, ovens, and mills for grinding corn. The other, at the foot of the cliff, had a tower two stories high. Wheat and vegetable seeds were planted in the surrounding fields, and within eight days the shoots sprang up through the fertile soil. The colony was named Charlesbourg Royal in honor of King Francis' son, Prince Charles.

On the seventeenth of September Cartier set out with two

longboats to make a quick survey of the route to the Kingdom of Saguenay. As he would pass the village of Achelacy on his way up the St. Lawrence, he took with him a cloak of "Paris red," trimmed with shining bells and buttons. This was a present for the Chief of Achelacy who had let his little daughter go with Cartier to France. She had remained there when Cartier returned to Canada, we do not know why. Nor do we know what explanation Cartier gave her father. But the chief appeared to be satisfied with the news he received. He welcomed Cartier like a long-lost brother and agreed to take two French boys into his tribe to learn the Indian language.

After Cartier left Achelacy, the records of his voyage become more and more incomplete. When he reached Montreal, he succeeded in crossing the first rapid, the St. Mary's Current, by double-manning one of his longboats. Then he proceeded with this single boat to the second rapid, the Lachine, which he could not cross because the current was too swift and the rocks too dangerous.

Afterward he continued by foot along a path on the River's bank. He met a band of Indians and asked them how far the rapids were from one another. The Indians laid little sticks on the ground and indicated that the distance from the foot of the first rapid to the head of the third and last was about sixteen leagues, or fifteen miles by land. "And the Kingdom of Saguenay?" asked Cartier. "Can the Kingdom be reached by water?"

The Indians said that this was impossible and thus denied Chief Donnacona's words: "The usual route to the Kingdom of Saguenay is by way of the Ottawa River."

Winter was closing in on Cartier, and he could reconnoiter no farther that year. There was another reason for his wishing to leave Montreal as soon as possible: he was no longer sure of the Indians' real feeling toward him. They had appeared to be glad

to see him and to enjoy his gifts. But he himself said later, "A man must not trust those Indians for all their fair ceremonies and signs of joy for if they had thought that they had been too strong for us, then they would have done their best to kill us, as we understood afterward."

Cartier was now paying dearly for the lies which he had told the Quebec Indians, who must have learned, while he was away reconnoitering, that all the tribesmen whom he had seized and carried off to France were dead. Probably runners had been sent from Quebec to warn the other tribes that Cartier himself could not be trusted.

He left Montreal without delay and on his way down the River stopped at Achelacy. The two young Frenchmen who had stayed there to learn the Indian language told him that the Chief of Achelacy, who had been Cartier's one real friend in Canada, had gone to Quebec to join Agona in preparing for a war against the French.

When Cartier reached his colony at Charlesbourg Royal, he sent scouts to Quebec, and they brought back word that the Indians were gathering there in hostile masses. He immediately ordered the forts to be strengthened. Then the story of his Indian adventures comes to an abrupt end; all records of what really happened during that winter have been lost.

Spring came, the ice broke in the St. Lawrence River, and still Lord de Roberval had not arrived with reinforcements. Whether or not there had been real fighting between Cartier and the Indians, we do not know. Nor do we know if scurvy had again ravaged the colony. But it is evident that, lacking supplies, Cartier could no longer keep his discouraged men in the wilderness. He must sail back to France without having reached the Kingdom of Saguenay. But he hoped that the "nuggets of gold and the diamonds" which had been found near the Cap Rouge River might make up for the failure.

He gathered together his surviving men, trimmed his sails, and headed homeward. He chose the shorter passage to the Atlantic, by way of the south coast of Newfoundland. There, by chance, in St. John's Harbor, he met Lord de Roberval, who had just arrived with three tall ships and two hundred colonists. Lord de Roberval was strutting like a conqueror; he wore gleaming armor and a plumed helmet, his standard was decorated with a cross.

Cartier reported to Lord de Roberval and showed him the "nuggets of gold and the diamonds." The sailors built a furnace to test the ore, and the results appeared to be satisfactory. Then Roberval ordered Cartier to accompany the new expedition to Charlesbourg Royal. But Cartier refused to do so because he had not been engaged to serve indefinitely, and he had already suffered enough from the delays and inefficiency of this commander. Cartier gave Roberval directions for reaching Charlesbourg Royal and afterward, in the darkness of the night, slipped away to France.

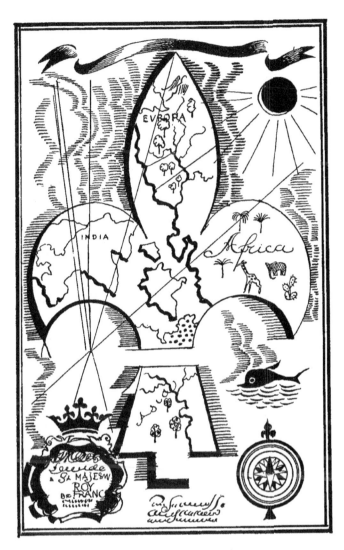

THE FAME OF
JACQUES CARTIER

When the "gold and diamonds" were tested in France, they proved to be copper and mica. A saying sprang into usage: *False as a diamond of Canada,* and the laughter and mockery that followed brought Cartier's career as an explorer to an end. Lord de Roberval returned to France in 1543 after having failed miserably both with his colony and in his attempts to find the riches of Saguenay. Then King Francis abandoned Canada to the Indians.

No explorer ever found the fabulous riches of the Kingdom of Saguenay. Those tales of rubies and pearls, of silver and gold and spices, and of men who flew like bats had been invented by Chief Donnacona. They were somewhat like the Indian stories of Quivira, the golden city, which the Spanish explorer Coronado had tried to find in Arizona and New Mexico. They were like the legend told by South American Indians about El Dorado, the golden king, and the golden lake which Europeans would seek vainly for many years to come.

Between the Indian tales of fabulous riches and the old medieval legends which French people still loved, there was little room for Cartier's plain and accurate descriptions of Canada which were printed from his logbooks. Kings and commoners alike preferred to read the works of an author like Thevet, the royal cosmographer, who collected fantastic stories about the Americas. Thevet interviewed Chief Donnacona and published much of what the chief said, not only about the riches in Saguenay, but also about the pygmies and one-legged men supposed to have inhabited that marvelous country.

And Thevet, even after he had talked with Cartier, wrote the following description of an Isle of Demons near Newfoundland:

True it is and I myself have heard it, not from one but from a great number of sailors and pilots with whom I have made many voyages, that, when they passed this way they heard in the air, on the tops and about the masts, a great clamor of men's voices, confused and inarticulate, such as you may hear from the crowd at a fair or market place.

Probably Thevet's most amazing creation was a map of the world which he drew in the shape of a fleur-de-lis.

Cartier spent the last years of his life quietly in St. Malo. Mapmakers and geographers sometimes traveled there to consult him, for they understood the value of his explorations and the contribution which he had made to human knowledge. But although Cartier had claimed the Canadian wilderness for France, he died in St. Malo in 1557 without having received the public recognition due him for his service to his country. Few people in the sixteenth century understood that the St. Lawrence River was a source of wealth more enduring than gold mines.

Not until the early seventeenth century did France begin to appreciate Cartier's colonial plan. Then, in 1608, another Frenchman, Samuel Champlain, set sail for Canada and founded a permanent settlement at Quebec, not far from the site of Chief Donnacona's former village. Later other settlements sprang up on the banks and the islands of the River. And from these settlements went hunters, trappers, traders, and brave and saintly priests who carried a new civilization into the wilderness that Cartier had discovered.